SLEEP-EASY
INVESTING

Also by Gordon Pape

INVESTMENT ADVICE

The Retirement Time Bomb

Get Control of Your Money

6 Steps to $1 Million

Retiring Wealthy in the 21st Century

The Complete Guide to RRIFs and LIFs (with David Tafler)

Gordon Pape's 2004 Buyer's Guide to Mutual Funds (with Eric Kirzner)

Gordon Pape's 2004 Buyer's Guide to RRSPs

Secrets of Successful Investing (with Eric Kirzner)

Gordon Pape's Investing Strategies 2001 (with Richard Croft and Eric Kirzner)

Making Money in Mutual Funds

The Canadian Mortgage Book (with Bruce McDougall)

The Best of Pape's Notes

Head Start (with Frank Jones)

Retiring Wealthy

Building Wealth in the '90s

Low-Risk Investing in the '90s

Low-Risk Investing

Building Wealth

CONSUMER ADVICE

Gordon Pape's International Shopping Guide (with Deborah Kerbel)

HUMOUR

The $50,000 Stove Handle

CHRISTMAS (with Deborah Kerbel)

Quizmas Carols

Family Quizmas

Quizmas: Christmas Trivia Family Fun
(www.quizmas.net)

FICTION (with Tony Aspler)

Chain Reaction

The Scorpion Sanction

The Music Wars

NON-FICTION

Montreal at the Crossroads (with Donna Gabeline and Dane Lanken)

SLEEP-EASY INVESTING

Your Stress-Free
Guide to
Financial Success

Gordon Pape

VIKING
CANADA

VIKING CANADA

Published by the Penguin Group

Penguin Group (Canada), 90 Eglinton Avenue East, Suite 700, Toronto, Ontario, Canada
M4P 2Y3 (a division of Pearson Canada Inc.)

Penguin Group (USA) Inc., 375 Hudson Street, New York, New York 10014, U.S.A.
Penguin Books Ltd, 80 Strand, London WC2R 0RL, England
Penguin Ireland, 25 St Stephen's Green, Dublin 2, Ireland (a division of Penguin Books Ltd)
Penguin Group (Australia), 250 Camberwell Road, Camberwell, Victoria 3124, Australia
(a division of Pearson Australia Group Pty Ltd)
Penguin Books India Pvt Ltd, 11 Community Centre, Panchsheel Park, New Delhi – 110 017,
India
Penguin Group (NZ), 67 Apollo Drive, Rosedale, North Shore 0632, New Zealand
(a division of Pearson New Zealand Ltd)
Penguin Books (South Africa) (Pty) Ltd, 24 Sturdee Avenue, Rosebank, Johannesburg 2196,
South Africa

Penguin Books Ltd, Registered Offices: 80 Strand, London WC2R 0RL, England

First published 2008

1 2 3 4 5 6 7 8 9 10 (RRD)

Copyright © Gordon Pape Enterprises Ltd., 2008

This publication contains the opinions and ideas of its author and is designed to provide useful
advice in regard to the subject matter covered. The author and publisher are not engaged in
rendering legal, accounting, or other professional services in this publication. This publication
is not intended to provide a basis for action in particular circumstances without consideration
by a competent professional. The author and publisher expressly disclaim any responsibility
for any liability, loss, or risk, personal or otherwise, which is incurred as a consequence,
directly or indirectly, of the use and application of any of the contents of this book.

Manufactured in the U.S.A.

ISBN-13: 978-0-670-06689-6
ISBN-10: 0-670-06689-3

LIBRARY AND ARCHIVES CANADA CATALOGUING IN PUBLICATION

Pape, Gordon, 1936–
Sleep-easy investing : your stress-free guide to financial success / Gordon Pape.

Includes bibliographical references and index.
ISBN 978-0-670-06689-6

1. Investments. I. Title.
HG4521.P353 2008   332.6   C2007-905661-X

Visit the Penguin Group (Canada) website at **www.penguin.ca**

Special and corporate bulk purchase rates available; please see
www.penguin.ca/corporatesales or call 1-800-810-3104, ext. 477 or 474

To all my faithful readers over the years, thank you.

Contents

SLEEP-EASY
INVESTING

Chapter 1

What's *Really* Important?

In investing money, the amount of interest you want should depend on whether you want to eat well or sleep well.
—J. Kenfield Morley

Before you start reading this book, I want you to ask yourself a simple question. It's this: What is your number one investment priority? If you've never stopped to think about it, now is the time.

Is your main goal to beat the market averages? Is it to find the next hot stock so you can double your money overnight? Is it to retire at age 50? Perhaps it's to make big profits so you can brag about them at cocktail parties, in which case you could be suffering from ego deprivation. More modestly, maybe you want nothing more than to earn 10 percent on your money every year.

Pause for a minute to consider your answer.

Got it?

Okay. If you said something like "to get rich" or if you found yourself nodding in agreement at any of my suggestions, you need to go off to a quiet corner and rethink your whole approach to money management.

Why? Because the number one goal of every investor should actually be to sleep comfortably at night.

Sounds simplistic? Sure it is! Is it easy? Absurdly so. And I promise you this: If you adopt my Sleep-Easy investing philosophy as your own and make all future financial decisions based on how well they meet the Sleep-Easy test, both your health and your wealth will benefit.

Here's your starting point. Beginning right now, whenever you are faced with a financial decision, ask yourself: "Is this likely to cause me any regrets down the road?" If the answer is "yes" or even "possibly," pass. There are lots of other places for your money.

I get emails all the time from people who didn't take this approach when faced with a major financial decision and ended up deeply regretting it. One came from a couple in their early 60s who had been persuaded to take out a home equity line of credit and invest the money in mutual funds. They were down $10,000 within the first three months. The wife was desperate to bail out, even though it would cost them thousands of dollars in deferred sales charges on top of their capital loss. The husband wanted to stick it out. How well do you suppose those folks were sleeping at night? What kind of conversations were they having at the dinner table? Who needs that kind of aggravation?—life is tough enough.

Another email came from a man who had ignored all the warnings about aggressive tax shelters, including official press releases from the Canada Revenue Agency (CRA). Instead, he put a lot of money in a questionable scheme that promised to send him a charitable donation receipt for an amount far in excess of what he actually paid. He contacted me after his deduction had been disallowed by the CRA and he had been served notice that his account would be audited. As you might expect, he was desperate and was hoping I could come up with some miracle advice that would bail him out.

No such luck—he'd made his own bed and now the tax people were going to make him lie in it. It was a tough lesson learned. But if he had applied the Sleep-Easy test at the time, he would have avoided all the misery.

Many of us have bought stocks that we knew little about, on the basis of a tip from a friend or a persuasive broker because, we were assured, it was about to take off. In most cases, "crash land" would have been a more accurate prediction. Using the Sleep-Easy test before making the purchase would have saved both worry and money.

Over the decades that I have been writing about money, I've met and communicated with thousands of people. I can honestly say that very few—perhaps 5 percent at best—have a rational approach to handling money. The rest fall into three main camps.

The Greedy. These folks approach investing in the same way they would play a Las Vegas slot machine. They keep feeding in money and pressing the buttons in the hope that they'll hit the jackpot and become an instant millionaire. They're also the same people who tie up the checkout at the local convenience store for 20 minutes while they decide which lottery tickets to buy.

These are the people who are most likely to get into big trouble because they can't resist a sales pitch. Sit them down at a desk and explain how they can put their cash into a sure thing and earn fat profits overnight, and they'll bite every time. They can't see any potential downside risk because they're too convinced that the big score is just around the corner.

The Blissfully Ignorant. These people don't pay any attention to money—until they suddenly find themselves in deep doo-doo. They spend virtually every cent they earn, and when they do save a little, they typically toss it into an RRSP to get the tax break without bothering to ask what the money will be invested in. They're the ones who complain to me years later that their retirement savings have hardly grown at all. You have to wonder what they expected from a 3 percent guaranteed investment certificate.

I am always amazed at the number of people who really don't want to know what's happening to their money. A couple of years ago, I received an email from a woman who said she was in her mid-50s. She had lost half the money in her investment account and asked my advice on where to put what was left so that she didn't have to pay any attention to it.

My answer was: "If you had taken the trouble to learn a little about investing and paid attention to what was happening, you wouldn't have lost half your money. You would have reacted quickly when you saw what was happening and done something about it. If you want to invest, for heaven's sake, devote a little time to learning about it. How much time do you spend researching when you buy a television set?"

Blissfully ignorant folks may sleep well for a time, but it is the sleep of naïveté. At one point, they wake up in a panic, as was the case here. By then it's often too late to fill in the financial hole they've dug for themselves.

The Fearful. These people don't sleep well because they're always afraid. If they put their money in a bank, they worry that the bank will go belly up. If they bury it in the backyard, they worry the dog will dig it up. If they keep it under the mattress, it creates uncomfortable lumps.

Of course, I'm exaggerating here but only to emphasize the point. The Sleep-Easy philosophy does not involve fretting over every aspect of your financial life. On the contrary, my approach is designed to eliminate financial worries almost entirely. Kids, sex, global warming, and health provide enough issues to be anxious about. I want you to take money off that list.

Granted, you can always find plenty of financial issues to worry about if you put your mind to it. There's always something in the headlines to set your nerves on edge. For example, as I write this book, North American stock markets are hitting record highs. You'd think everyone would be rejoicing, but no. Gasoline prices have climbed to over a dollar a litre, leaving consumers grumbling and politicians threatening action against the big, bad energy companies. The Bank of Canada is warning that interest rates will have to start rising again because of inflation concerns, causing jitters in the bond markets and tension in families that are already overextended on their mortgage payments. The Canadian dollar is posting 30-year highs, which may be good news for snowbirds but is causing widespread angst among our manufacturers. In the United States, the business press is lamenting the collapse of the subprime housing market and warning of its implications for that country's lacklustre economy. Even in boom times, we can find things to keep us awake if we try hard enough.

Of course, when things are bad, as they were during the millennium bear market that kicked off this century, losing sleep is simple—just watch the news right before going to bed and you're guaranteed a night of tossing and turning, with a few nightmares mixed in once you do manage to drift off. But what if I told you that I know people who slept soundly every night right through those tough three years? Why? Because while most people were watching their net worth dwindle away, they were actually becoming richer—not because they had gambled, but because they hadn't. They were therefore immune to the hair-trigger tension created by the plunging stock market.

So what does it take to become a Sleep-Easy investor? That's what this book is all about, but I'll give you a sneak preview right now.

Balance. The ancient Greeks understood that moderation in all things is the key to contentment. Euripides went so far as to call it "the noblest gift of heaven." Well, that's certainly true when it comes to money. Taking a balanced approach to investing is the single most important thing you can do to guarantee yourself a good night's sleep. It sounds easy, but I can assure you it is not. You have to work hard at it. I'll explain how later in the book.

Common sense. I can't count the number of times people have come to me with screwball ideas about how to make money. Here's one example. I offer a free question-and-answer service on my website at www.buildingwealth.ca. Recently, a young man sent in this query:

> *I was told I should invest in a non-registered money market fund using my line of credit and pay the monthly interest charged by the bank. Just before the RRSP deadline in the following year, I should terminate my investment account, pay off my line of credit, and invest the excess earnings into my RRSP. In addition, the interest I pay for my line of credit is tax deductible. Is this true?*

With no disrespect to the correspondent, it was immediately clear to me that he was so intrigued by the idea of making extra money while sticking it to the tax department that his common sense had gone right out the window. This is how I replied:

Yes, it's true. Whether it makes any sense is another matter. Let's apply a little math. The average Canadian money market fund returned 3.23 percent over the latest one-year period. Since interest rates are creeping up, let's assume that over the next 12 months you'll earn 3.5 percent. So for every $1,000 you invest, you'll receive $35 in interest.

The typical bank interest rate on a home equity line of credit is prime plus a quarter-point. If the line of credit is unsecured, it will be higher. The bank prime rate is currently 6 percent, so we'll assume you pay 6.25 percent on the loan. Over a year, you'll shell out $62.50 for every $1,000 you borrow.

As you have been told, the interest is tax deductible because you have used the money to invest. If your marginal tax rate is 40 percent, that means your after-tax interest cost per $1,000 borrowed will be reduced to $37.50.

But that is still more than you have earned on the money market fund. To make matters worse, the interest on the money fund is taxable. At a 40 percent rate, this means you'll be left with $21 in your pocket for every $1,000 invested.

So, you pay $37.50 per $1,000 invested to earn a net of $21. You'll never get rich that way. I suggest you think it through again.

If he had just used a little common sense, he would have figured this out for himself. Give him a little credit, though. At least he asked for someone else's advice before plunging ahead.

Attention to detail. I know people who suffer from what I call detail deficiency when it comes to money management. They can't stick to a budget, never manage to make ends meet, have zero savings, are always behind on paying their bills, and manage to run up big credit card debts without even realizing they're doing so.

If you are an incurable victim of detail deficiency, my advice is to hand complete responsibility for all financial matters to your spouse or partner. If you don't have one, or if he or she suffers from the same malady, hire a professional to look after your money. Yes, it will be an added expense, but believe me, it will be worth it.

> **SLEEP-EASY ADVICE:** Balance, common sense, and attention to detail are the keys to my Sleep-Easy philosophy. Of course, there is more to it than that; otherwise, I wouldn't have written an entire book on the subject. But those are the basic components. Think about the extent to which you've applied these three disciplines to managing your money until now—most people will come up short in at least one area—and then move on to the next chapter.

Chapter 2

Everyone's an Investor

More money has been made in real estate than in all industrial investments combined.
—Andrew Carnegie

Maybe you don't think of yourself as an investor. You wouldn't be alone. Most people just worry about having enough money to get by. Investing is the last thing on their minds—or so they think.

In reality, virtually everyone is an investor. Do you have an RRSP? Then you're an investor. Do you have an employer pension plan? You're an investor. Have you set up a registered education savings plan (RESP) for the kids? You're an investor. Do you own a home? You're an investor. Do you have a savings account? You're an investor.

The fact is that many Canadians are investors without even realizing it. That puts them into my Blissfully Ignorant category. Their financial future is taking shape somewhere in the deep background without them even being aware of what's going on, much less having any influence on it. As a result, they may be in a Sleep-Easy phase right now. But in a few years, that could change dramatically.

For example, many people are unaware of how the pension landscape is evolving around them, and not to their benefit. In the good old days, you went to work for a company, put in your time, paid into the pension plan, and then retired at age 65. The amount of your pension was determined by your years of service and your salary level, and it was guaranteed by the employer. Simple, neat, and, as it turns out, so outrageously expensive that some pension plan obligations have helped to drive major companies into bankruptcy.

We all know that America's Big Three automakers are on life support. It's not just because they have been making cars that fewer people want and have failed to learn from companies such as Toyota, which designs its vehicles to meet real human needs rather than to look flashy on a showroom floor. Sure, Detroit needs to reinvent itself if it is going to regain dominance in its home market. But it's trying to do so with one leg in a cast and a hand tied behind its back. Why? In large part because of the rich packages handed out to retirees over the years by General Motors, Ford, and Chrysler—benefits that were negotiated by the tough United Auto Workers union, which must shoulder part of the blame for the current mess, whether it admits it or not.

Pension commitments are part of the problem, but not the major issue at this point. Health care costs are the real killer, especially those paid to retirees. Ford estimates they add $1,200 to the cost of every car, while Chrysler puts its figure at $1,500, and General Motors at $1,600 (GM now supports three retirees to every active worker). In contrast, the average health care bill per vehicle for Toyota and Honda is $350.

All three of the big U.S. automakers have fully funded pension plans, although had General Motors CEO Rick Wagoner not injected US$18 billion into that company's pension fund in 2003, just as the stock market was starting to take off again, the story might be quite different. Indeed, some economists credit Wagoner's move with saving GM from bankruptcy.

But there's a hidden story here, one that affects a growing number of people in both the United States and Canada and which may lead to many sleepless nights in the years to come for those who don't recognize its significance and do something about it.

During the latter part of the 20th century, private-sector employers started to wake up to the fact that two converging forces could potentially jeopardize their very existence. One was the high cost of the retirement benefits packages they offered. The second was an aging population, characterized by the baby boom generation. Unless changes were made, demographic trends would eventually swamp corporations with retirement-related costs far in excess of their ability to pay. (In theory, the same problem exists in the public sector, but since retirement expenses there are funded in part by taxpayers, the issue has never been properly addressed.)

The response of the private sector has been to strip down retirement benefits of all types. In a survey published in June 2007, Aon Consulting reported that 55 percent of responding Canadian employers were considering phasing out health care benefits for retirees because of rising costs.

One of the main casualties of the cutbacks has been defined benefit pension plans (DBPPs)—those plans that guarantee a specific income at retirement age based on a set formula. Defined benefit plans are a great asset for anyone who wants a Sleep-Easy retirement, since they provide a steady and predictable income source that is sometimes indexed for inflation. But they are becoming increasingly rare because of the high cost of funding and administering them. As a result, some employers have shut down their defined benefit plans, and most new programs are either group RRSPs or defined contribution pension plans (DCPPs).

What does this have to do with Sleep-Easy investing? A lot. Group RRSPs and DCPPs may be corporate-sponsored, but they offer no guarantees at the end of the road. When you reach retirement age, the amount of the pension you receive will have little to do with how long you worked for the company or how high your salary was. Instead, the amount of pension you receive in your so-called golden years (which may end up being more leaden than golden) will be determined mainly by how well or poorly the investments in your pension plan or group RRSP performed over time. And that, my friends, will increasingly be your responsibility. You will have to decide how the money will be invested, and it will be a challenge.

How much of a challenge? Here's what one email I recently received from a reader said:

> My son, who is 30, has asked me for advice, but I'm not sure what to recommend. He has been given the opportunity to invest in two company-sponsored RRSP group plans. The first is operated by the Mackenzie Group, while the other is operated by Sun Life Financial. His company matches each dollar that he invests, up to 4 percent of his salary. He has given me the sales materials with all the various funds that both RRSP group plan providers offer, but there's just too much to choose from, so I'm not sure which fund(s) to recommend. Can you provide me with some advice, please?

Here's the problem: Both organizations provide so many choices that it is almost impossible for inexperienced people to decide where to put their money. At the time of writing, Sun Life had 275 listings covering all types of units on the Globefund.com website, which tracks the performance of Canadian mutual funds. Most Sun Life products are based on funds managed by another organization, such as CI Investments. In one sense, it's good to have a lot of choice. However, as the saying goes, you can have too much of a good thing. Now, in all probability, the Sun Life list offered to my correspondent's son was somewhat smaller, but based on his comments, it was still confusing enough to prompt an appeal for help.

The Mackenzie Financial lineup is smaller, but not by much. When I checked, it had 221 Globefund entries from which to choose, more than enough to send even a seasoned investor into a catatonic trance. The saving grace is that it is somewhat easier to navigate because it is divided into several families (e.g., Cundill, Ivy, Maxxum, Sentinel, Universal), each of which takes a distinctive approach to choosing securities. So someone looking for conservative mutual funds could focus on the Cundill and Ivy offerings, while those seeking greater growth potential might zero in on the Universal funds.

The point is that there are decisions to be made that will have a major impact on a family's future. And in this case the decision-making responsibility fell to a 30-year-old who probably has minimal (if any) investing experience and had to turn to Dad for guidance. For his part, Dad didn't have a clue what to suggest.

If you think this is an isolated case, think again. Every day, thousands of Canadians are being asked to make similar decisions about their retirement savings, often with little or no understanding of the options or the longer-term implications.

Some companies are offering professional guidance in an effort to ease the inevitable stress. But in too many cases, the employees are left to cope on their own. They're handed a sheaf of papers, which they are asked to complete and return. Among them will probably be a personal investment profile and a sheet on which they are asked to indicate how they want their pension savings allocated. Whether they like it or not, they've become investors.

Now let's consider the family home. For many years, I advised people not to consider it as an investment but, rather, as simply a place to live. If it could eventually be sold for a profit, that would be all well and good. But the main concern should be buying a property where your family could be comfortable and happy.

Again, those were simpler times. In today's market, your home is a huge investment, one that could eventually provide a large chunk of your retirement income. Escalating property values have allowed people to downsize after the kids have left home, pocketing hundreds of thousands of dollars in capital gains in the process. Since your primary residence is tax-exempt in Canada, this is all found money. Every cent of profit stays in your pocket.

Even people who decide not to sell are monetizing the value of their home. Reverse mortgages and lines of credit allow people to tap into their home equity to generate cash flow or to access money for renovations, investing, travel, or whatever. Home is where the heart is? Not any more. "Home is where the cash is" would be more accurate.

Of course, your home is likely where you sleep most of the time. But you may not rest easy if you have mismanaged what is probably the biggest single investment you will ever make. And there are lots of ways to do that, unfortunately. Here are a few.

Overpaying. When property markets are hot, it's easy to succumb to buyers' panic, and real estate agents do their best to encourage it. You see a house that you like, and you're inevitably told that you need to act fast because there's another offer coming in. You may even be advised to submit a bid that's higher than the asking price to be sure you get the place. It happens all the time.

When it comes to buying a home, emotion is a luxury you cannot afford. It can end up costing you thousands of dollars. Never allow yourself to fall in love with a property to the point of convincing yourself that no other will do. There will always be others. And don't be pressured into making an overly generous offer. If you can't get the house at a reasonable price, pass.

Overextending. Most people have a top dollar amount in mind when they set out to buy a home. That's good. The problem arises when they allow themselves to be pushed over that limit, sometimes by tens of thousands of dollars.

Remember that most real estate agents are paid by commission. That means the higher the dollar value of the sale, the more they collect. They have an incentive to encourage you to stretch beyond your limit, as long as the mortgage will be approved. Some less scrupulous agents will take advantage of the situation. There are several ways to do this. One is to show you undesirable properties that are priced within the range you have set. Now, these houses may be grossly overpriced, but you are not told that. Instead, the agent says that to find the kind of place you really want, you have to be prepared to spend more. The agent can make a convincing argument, even as he or she empathizes with you about the cost.

The way to beat this ploy is to insist that the price range you have set is firm. Be businesslike, and don't budge. If the agent doesn't show you anything you like, scan the classifieds for private sales in your price range. Attend open houses on your own. Consider finding another agent. Unless you are being totally unrealistic, you'll eventually find a place you like and that's affordable.

Aggressive refinancing. Over the past decade or so, we've seen the emergence of an unhealthy financial phenomenon that undercuts personal worth. It's the increasingly popular trend to resort to refinancing as a means of getting out of financial trouble. Here's how it works.

As property values rise, homeowners' equity increases. In fast-growth areas such as Toronto, Calgary, and Vancouver, even a modest property might rise in value by $50,000 to $100,000 over a few years. That money can be tapped into by refinancing the mortgage.

Most financial institutions will gladly comply with such requests, since mortgage loans are one of their safest sources of income (Canadians rarely default). All that's involved is a new appraisal, a rate adjustment if the mortgage term isn't up, and your signature on a few forms. Presto, you have thousands of dollars added to your bank account, to spend as you want. Unfortunately, in many cases the money has to be used to pay down credit card debt or is frittered away.

Refinancing may seem like a great source of ready cash, but in fact what it does is increase your debt load, raise your monthly mortgage payment, and reduce your net worth. Once you realize that the bank didn't really give you money for nothing—even though it seemed that way at the time—you may come to the conclusion that perhaps it wasn't such a great idea after all.

Buying or selling at the wrong time. Of course, you should never buy a house at the top of the market and never sell at the bottom. But, as with the stock market, the temptation is often to do exactly that. For buyers, there is the fear that a rising market will run away from them if they don't move fast. During a real estate slump, sellers start to believe that the market will never recover and so slash prices in desperation.

Always remember that real estate markets are cyclical. Prices don't keep rising in a straight line; sooner or later they will pull back. It may seem hard to believe now, but back in the 1980s the housing market in Alberta got so bad that people were walking away from their properties because the amount due on the mortgage exceeded the resale value. Imagine how those folks feel now.

A variation on this blunder is the "buying before selling" gaffe. An email I received shows where that can lead:

I hope you can help us. We are in trouble with our finances. We are planning to set up our own business this year. My husband has to quit his job. We bought a house in a small city, planning to sell our old house in Vancouver to cover our cost of the new house.... We got our friend who is an agent to sell it. But that didn't work out so then we changed to an agent who gets only 1 percent commission. We brought down the price of [our] house and we had a good offer, but our friends said we should get more than that, so we did not sell. Recently we got another offer, but the price was too low and we did not accept it.

Now we have to pay a mortgage on two houses, and my husband has no job. If we can not sell our old house within two months, we may have a problem.... The house is located in a very good area, the price is in the [right] range, so why can't we sell it? Please give us any suggestions and help you can. We have two kids.

Unfortunately, this mess was very much of the couple's own making. The first rule of switching houses is to not buy a new one before the old one is sold. Otherwise, the risk is that you'll end up in exactly the position in which this couple found themselves: carrying two mortgages at the same time.

In fact, this couple made all kinds of mistakes. To start with, they hired a friend as their real estate agent. Selling a home is a major business transaction, but they did not treat it that way. Then they decided to try to sell the house on the cheap. An agent who charges a 1 percent commission is probably not going to be highly motivated to spend a lot of time working on the file, and I would guess that the home was not on the Multiple Listing Service. The couple's next mistake was turning down a decent offer because their friends were critical of it. They should have ignored them—after all, the friends didn't have to foot the bill for the two mortgages.

One of the cardinal rules in real estate is to not let a house sit on the market for too long. If it doesn't sell within a few weeks, it becomes stale goods—the people who might be interested have looked at it, rejected it for whatever reason, and moved on.

I told this couple that they appeared to have only two options, neither of them particularly good. One was to take the house off the market and rent it for a year or so. That would provide the money they needed to carry the mortgage, as well as a tax write-off and perhaps a small profit. They could then relist the house with a major real estate company. The commission would be higher, but the chances of a sale would increase dramatically.

The second option was to drastically reduce the asking price. There is always a buyer—if the price is low enough. But they would probably have to accept a lot less money than they had hoped for.

As I told them, it's a tough call, but you're in a tough spot. I subsequently received a reply from them in which they acknowledged that they were the authors of their own misfortune. "It is true this mess is very much our own mistake," the wife wrote. "Now we have to move on. Our agent/friend started to complain to us that we did not make our own decisions. That is the lesson we need to learn—to not let anybody influence us. Another lesson we learned was to sell the house first, before buying another one."

Unfortunately, it was an expensive way to get an education in real estate economics.

> **SLEEP-EASY ADVICE:** We are all investors in one way or another. It's essential to realize that and to understand that the decisions we make today will have a profound effect on our future financial well-being, and on how well we sleep later.

Chapter 3

Sex and Money

Money, it turned out, was exactly like sex; you thought of nothing else if you didn't have it and thought of other things if you did.
—James Baldwin

Studies have repeatedly shown that sex and money are the two main sources of conflict in marriages. By extension, that implies they are the primary reasons why people lose sleep at night.

We all know from experience that good sex usually leads to a good night's sleep. Well, so does good money. Remove the stress of financial concerns from your life and you'll be amazed at what it does for your sleeping habits. Throw away the pills!

Just as there are a variety of sexual tensions, there are several forms of financial stress. Let's take a look at four of them and consider ways to deal with them.

Not having enough. This one is universal. No one, except maybe Bill Gates and Warren Buffett, has enough money. No matter how high your income, it never seems to be quite adequate to make ends meet. There's a simple reason for this: Expectations always exceed returns. To put it another way, the more we get, the more we want. A starving man will treasure a few crusts of bread, while a wealthy man will have them trimmed off his sandwich. Condemn that attitude if you want, but nonetheless it is part of human nature.

Many years ago, when I was a teenager, I asked my father how much money was "enough." I have never forgotten his reply: "Only you can answer that. It all depends on how you want to live." Now that I'm supposedly rich, I fully understand what he meant. My story is similar to that of many other people, and I think it clearly illustrates the "never enough" syndrome.

I began life with virtually nothing in the way of financial resources. Neither my wife nor I came from wealthy families, and when we married, in 1962, we couldn't even afford to go on a honeymoon. We lived in a rented apartment in a lower-middle-class area of Montreal and, because we both worked, we scraped by. But there was never enough money for anything beyond the basics.

Over the years, as my income increased, our lifestyle changed accordingly. After a few promotions and our first child, we decided to stretch our budget to the limit and buy a $45,000 house in the west end of Ottawa. Because my wife had quit her job to care for the baby, we found ourselves in the same position as many young homeowners: house poor. We had more wealth in that we were now property owners, but we didn't have any more cash available for travel, dining out, or saving.

That pattern continued for many years as we moved from Ottawa to London, England, to Montreal to Toronto. Something always happened to perpetuate the "never enough" syndrome. At one point, just when we were starting to get our heads above the financial waters, the company for which I worked decided to transfer its operations from Montreal to Toronto. We sold our suburban Montreal home for $75,000, only to turn around and invest almost twice that amount in a smaller property in Toronto. Once again, we were house poor.

It took many years to get out from under. But by the time I reached my early 60s, we were in decent financial shape. Were we satisfied? No! Instead, we decided to fulfill a lifelong dream by buying a winter home in Florida, paying far more than we originally budgeted or could reasonably afford (a typical home-buying error, as noted in the previous chapter). Suddenly, we were house poor again, and we got poorer as the Canadian dollar plunged to US$0.62 and the cost of carrying the Florida property climbed accordingly. Had it not been for the turnaround in the loonie that began in 2003, we probably would have had no choice but to sell.

Expectations that exceed returns = "never enough."

It's a formula to remember. The only way to beat it is by scaling back your expectations to a level somewhat below your income. That's counter to human nature, you say? My point exactly.

Foolish spending. Often the "never enough" syndrome is exacerbated by the imprudent allocation of available resources. That's a polite way of saying "spending your money foolishly." We are all guilty of it at times.

Consider this true story. A family, which shall remain anonymous, bought some guinea pigs for the education and amusement of their young children. After a few years, one of the guinea pigs became ill. Now these creatures have a short lifespan to begin with. (I'm no expert on the subject, but I have been told four years is about average.) However, this particular guinea pig was much loved by one of the children, so it was taken to a vet.

The vet dutifully examined the animal and declared that an X-ray was required. The X-ray revealed a tumour. The prognosis was that the guinea pig would die unless surgery was performed. Cost: $1,000.

Most people would throw up their hands at that point and sit the youngster down to explain the realities of life and death. But these parents saw the pleading look in the child's eyes and decided to go ahead. The operation was an apparent success—until four days later, when the guinea pig died. No refund from the vet, of course. Money that could have been used to pay down the credit card balance or make an RRSP contribution or buy new clothes for the kids was gone.

It's not just young people who make such mistakes. Here's an email I recently received from a couple in British Columbia.

> *My husband and I are both in our late 40s and are way behind what we should have saved by now for RRSPs. We would like to be able to enjoy the money now rather than waiting for retirement, not knowing (1) if we'll be around then or (2) if we are, what our health will be like.*
>
> *We own a home but would like to have an in-ground pool installed. We are looking to get advice re potentially withdrawing a large amount (perhaps $50,000) from our RRSP to pay for the pool plus whatever is left over toward the income tax that will be required for withdrawing. We do not want to take out a loan, as we have enough to pay down at the moment. Is this an extremely stupid idea?*

Now, I would never presume to call anyone's idea "extremely stupid." Let's just say that I can think of many better ways they could use the money, including leaving it where it is.

While it's true that no one knows what the future will bring, the odds are that both of these people will be around well into their

80s. The life expectancy for a man in the 45-to-49 age group is 34.3 years, while for a woman it is 38.5 years. As for health, unless there is a family history of serious disease or early death, the chances are they'll be active for most or all of that time.

Now, I admit that a pool is great fun—we have one in Florida. But an outdoor pool can be comfortably used only for about five months of the year, maximum, in Canada. Some people might decide that's worth withdrawing $50,000 from an RRSP. I'm not one of them.

Moreover, when you're thinking about something like this, you need to calculate not just the present cost but the future value of the money. Assuming 25 years to retirement and an average annual return of 7 percent, that $50,000 would grow to about $270,000, even if this couple never put another cent into the RRSP. That's the real cost to their retirement savings of going the pool route.

We all face the temptation to spend our money foolishly from time to time. My advice is to resist it. I know that the family who paid for the guinea pig surgery wish that they had it all to do over.

Debt. Charles Dickens, who despite his great popularity had financial worries all his life, put these words into the mouth of chronic debtor Wilkins Micawber in his semi-autobiographical novel *David Copperfield:* "Annual income twenty pounds, annual expenditure nineteen nineteen and six, result happiness. Annual income twenty pounds, annual expenditure twenty pounds ought and six, result misery."

Or, as our parents would say: "Live within your means."

Few of us do, which is why personal debt levels in North America are at the highest levels in history. The buy now, pay later approach, fuelled by easily accessible credit, has led many people into Micawber's hell of financial misery.

The simple solution is to devise a family budget that pegs spending at 90 percent of after-tax income and stick to it. But in the real world, the concept seems to present an insurmountable challenge to most families. There's always something that knocks the budget out of kilter—the car needs repair, or the kids have to go to camp, or the toilet overflows, or the air conditioner breaks down. In fact, you can beat those unexpected expenses by doing what governments do: Add an amount for contingencies to the budget. Hardly anyone does.

I agree that budgeting is not easy, and it's boring. Do it anyway. It's a necessary first step along the Sleep-Easy path. This is the formula you want to apply:

Returns that exceed expectations = financial comfort.

If you can reach that point, you'll be able to start saving money for education, retirement, or whatever. That's when smart investing kicks in.

Losing it. As we get older, we should be accumulating personal wealth. Ironically, this can often happen not by working harder but by doing nothing. Any homeowner will tell you that. The house you bought 10 years ago is probably worth twice as much today—perhaps more, depending on where you live. That's added tens or maybe hundreds of thousands of dollars to your net worth. You didn't have to do anything for that, other than maintain the place while you lived in it and keep up with the property taxes.

The RRSP that you opened years ago so as to get the tax refund may also have been quietly increasing in value over time. Even if you put only $1,000 a year into it and the money grew at a modest 5 percent annually, the plan would be worth almost $48,000 after 25 years. Plus, there is the possibility that you will receive a substantial inheritance as parents pass on, leaving behind their homes, savings, and insurance policies.

The upshot is that if you manage to avoid the debt trap, you could be worth a lot of money by the time you reach your mid-50s. Now the biggest financial worry becomes losing it. Life is full of ironies, and this is another one. Until now, you've fretted about not having enough money or going deeply into debt. Now you're worried because you finally have all you need (or so you think), and you don't want to blow it.

I've observed a rather strange response to this fear. Many people decide that the best way to protect their assets is not to spend money on anything frivolous. So they don't take the world cruise they've always talked about, or don't join a golf club, or don't buy a Florida condo. They protect their money by crimping their lifestyle.

Earlier in this chapter, I made the point that foolish spending should be avoided, so I can't be overly critical of this approach beyond pointing out that in these cases people do have the means to indulge in some luxuries but choose not to spend the money. The folly lies in the fact that often people, who are intent on preserving their nest egg by not spending it, commit the cardinal sin of investing their assets in high-risk securities, with the expectation of enhanced returns. When the stock market goes into a dive, they lose thousands, and their stress level climbs. Personally, I'd rather spend the money on a cruise.

SLEEP-EASY ADVICE: By reducing investment expectations, you also reduce risk, which in turn diminishes stress. Your nest egg will grow at a more modest rate, but it *will* grow. Knowing that may make it easier to indulge yourself once in a while, by spending a little extra.

Chapter 4

The Twin Demons: Fear and Greed

I will tell you the secret of getting rich on Wall Street: You try to be greedy when others are fearful and you try to be very fearful when others are greedy.
—Warren Buffett

There are only two emotions that matter as far as the stock market is concerned: fear and greed. They are the twin demons that drive markets up or down, depending on which is in ascendancy at any given time. Within the past decade, we've been able to observe both of them at work and to see how damaging they can be.

Greed was in total control in the dying years of the 20th century as the dot-com frenzy created a boom that was reminiscent of some of the greatest bubbles in history. Despite warnings from high-profile personalities such as then–U.S. Federal Reserve Board chairman Alan Greenspan, who cautioned the world against "irrational exuberance," many people lost all touch with reality. The internet, which few people had even heard of at the start of the 1990s, was suddenly seen as one of the greatest inventions of all time, a source of potentially huge profits. Everyone wanted to be part of the financial bonanza that was anticipated. Stocks of almost every internet company skyrocketed, even if the business was bleeding red ink. All that entrepreneurs needed was a good story to attract megabucks. Few people paid any attention to business plans and, in truth, no one had the experience to produce plausible profit-and-loss forecasts because the industry was still in its birth stage. Imaginations were free to run wild, and they did.

Just how insane did things get? Take a look at the 10-year chart of the NASDAQ Composite Index from mid-1997 to mid-2007. It resembles a seismographic recording of an earthquake. The index bumps along at around the 2,000 level until mid-1998 when it suddenly takes off, climbing all the way to the 5,000 mark in the early part of 1999. At that point, it plunges back to below 4,000 in the space of a few months. A couple of aftershocks take it back over 4,000 temporarily, but then the big slide takes hold. By the following spring, it is back at the 2,000 level, and it continued to bounce around in that range for the next six years.

The losses suffered by investors were horrendous. I don't have to repeat the gory details here; they have been well documented, and many readers will have painful memories of the carnage. My point is that this is a classic example of greed triumphant. It was the modern-day version of the Klondike gold rush. Everyone wanted to grab a pick (or in this case, a stock) and try to get rich quick.

A few sane voices spoke out in the midst of all this turmoil, but they were ignored. One of them was money manager Francis Chou, who a few years later would be named as fund manager of the decade by his peers. At the time, however, his funds were underperforming because he refused to allow himself to get caught

NASDAQ Composite (COMP-1)

up in the mania. Here's an excerpt from his comments to unitholders in his 1999 Chou Funds annual report:

> I'm alarmed by the cavalier way in which people invest in technology stocks; the thought process they are using is a subversion of the investment process. The rise of a stock price for a period of time is by no means an indicator of value, nor is it an assurance that we are looking at a "can't miss" investment. By all means take advantage of stock prices but do not get seduced by them! Paying 500 times for hot air is not an investment; it's pure speculation....
>
> Let's not play a fool's game by thinking that a stock can be bought at 100 times revenues and then proceed to hope,

against hope, that someone who is carried away by emotion, and is unaware of the risk involved, will buy it at 200 times revenues the following week. When the urge hits to make such a leap, take a cold shower until the inclination passes.[1]

In retrospect, of course, his comments turned out to be prophetic. But at the time, many people dismissed them as old-fashioned thinking. We were in a "new paradigm"—a term that's rarely heard these days. Stocks would rise for at least 10 years. It's amazing how greed can overwhelm reality.

And then fear decided it was its turn. The first hint of the market plunge to come appeared around Easter 2000 as stocks took a dive. But over the summer the markets rallied, and many people assumed the worst of the correction was over and that it had been largely confined to the high-tech sector. That turned out to be wishful thinking. The cancer was insidiously spreading to the broader market. The blue-chip Dow Jones Industrial Average held out the longest, not surprisingly, since large-cap stocks tend to be the last refuge in troubled times. For several months during 2000 and 2001, the Dow dipped below the 11,000 level, only to rally back, giving investors new hope. But the rot was eating away, and in late 2001 the Dow crumbled all the way to 8,000 as the September 11 attack on the World Trade Center triggered a huge sell-off.

After the immediate shock of the image of the collapsing towers began to recede, buyers came back into the market, snapping up what appeared to be bargains. By early 2002, the Dow was back over 10,000, and it appeared we were in a new bull market. In reality, it was a bear trap. The Dow went into freefall, dropping all the way to the 7,000 range by the fall. Investors panicked, and by September 2002 they were accepting almost any price they could get to bail out of their stocks. It wasn't quite 1929 all over again, but it came close. Fear was all-pervasive. The boundless optimism of 1999 had been replaced by a deep-seated gloom.

I believe that the millennium bear market left a deep and permanent scar on the psyche of the baby boomers. Many of them suffered heavy financial losses. In some cases, retirement plans had to be put on hold indefinitely as savings were decimated. As a result of that experience, many older people became reluctant to even consider going back into equities. Here's an example. It's from an email that was sent to me in early 2007, more than four years after the bear market ended.

> *After the last crash and having lost a considerable amount of money, I hesitate to get back into the mutual fund market. I feel that my financial planner did not do a very good job in sheltering my money against loss.*
>
> *Presently all of my money is in GICs. I know this is not the best place, as they are taxable, but fear keeps me there.*
>
> *I am in my 60s, and so you can see my reluctance to take a chance. What do you recommend for a nervous senior with cash to invest but very, very skeptical in this volatile market world?*

Keep in mind that this was written at a time when the S&P/TSX Composite Index, the S&P 500, and the Dow were posting new all-time highs. But the writer had been so traumatized by what happened in 2000–02 that he had sat on the sidelines with his money in GICs ever since, despite the fact that interest rates were near their lowest levels since the Second World War. It shows how fear can overwhelm financial common sense. The writer's nervousness had cost him the opportunity to recover all of his bear market losses and more. In fact, after taxes and inflation were taken into account, he probably lost even more money during the period by sitting in a supposedly safe investment.

In my response, I pointed out that there are many ways to reduce risk without opting out of the equity markets entirely. He could have put some of his money into a conservatively managed balanced fund and received a much higher return than GICs offered. I also noted that there were some stock funds that never lost money during the bear market—including those run by Francis Chou, which actually scored big gains during the period.

Of course, the past is history. All we can do is ignore it, bemoan it, or learn from it. As in other situations like this, where fear dominates all else, I suggested that he learn from his mistake and find a conservative financial advisor who would gradually shift some of the money out of GICs and into low-risk securities that offer somewhat higher returns. This doesn't mean abandoning GICs entirely—if they are held in tax-sheltered registered plans, they are a useful way to minimize risk. But I would suggest that, even for a nervous investor like this, GIC holdings should be 25 percent, tops, and I would never advise holding them in a non-registered portfolio because the interest attracts tax at a person's top marginal rate.

The older we get, the more likely it is that fear will overcome greed when it comes to investing. The self-described "nervous senior" who wrote the email I have been discussing was in his 60s and, in my experience, his attitude is fairly typical for his age group.

Younger people, especially those who have never faced heavy losses in a stock market crash, are more susceptible to the greed demon. Here's a question I received by email from a man in Guelph, Ontario, in the spring of 2007, a couple of weeks after the nervous senior sent his:

*I am 32 and have about $9,000 in mutual funds in my RRSP.
I would like to start investing in stocks by selling off my mutual
funds. Colleagues and friends of mine have done quite well
investing in five or six good dividend-paying stocks. Is this a
good idea?*

Consider the situation. Here's a young man who has been carefully building a small RRSP using mutual funds. But he'd been
talking to friends who appear to have chided him about his slow-
and-steady approach and boasted about the money they made in
the stock markets, which at the time were roaring ahead. Greed
had taken over, and he wanted some of that action too. But there
was a lingering doubt in his mind, which is why he wrote to me for
advice.

I counselled against changing his strategy, for several reasons.
For starters, his message suggested he had no experience in stock
market investing. That's just asking for trouble. As George
Goodman, who has written many great investment books under
the pseudonym of Adam Smith, once said: "If you don't know who
you are, the stock market is an expensive place to find out."

My second point was that people should never give too much
credence to the advice of friends when it comes to money, unless
they happen to be financial professionals—and even then, caution
is required. His buddies may have been doing well in stocks at the
time, but so was almost everyone else. A bull market had been in
place since 2003, and the rising tide had lifted everyone's boat. Ask
them how they fared between 2000 and 2002, I suggested.

Third, the amount of money he had available to invest in stocks
was very low—something less than $9,000. Blue chip stocks are
not cheap—Royal Bank, for example, traded for more than $50 a
share at the time. Diversification is one of the keys to stock market

success. He already had that in his mutual funds. With so little cash available, it would be impossible to properly diversify a personal stock portfolio.

Finally, he was talking about RRSP money. An RRSP is simply a mini-pension plan and should be treated accordingly. No professional pension fund manager in his or her right mind would consider investing all assets in the stock market—in fact, most would limit equity exposure to 50 or 60 percent, depending on conditions.

This was clearly a situation in which reason needed to triumph over greed. Unfortunately, I never heard back from him, so I cannot say with certainty that it did. Perhaps his pals persuaded him not to pay any attention to cautious old guys like me.

SLEEP-EASY ADVICE: If you allow either greed or fear to dominate your approach to investing, you will never sleep easy. You'll be tempted to succumb to both many times during your life. Resist! They'll bring nothing but trouble.

Chapter 5

The Price of Ignorance

Ignorance is not bliss—it is oblivion.
—Philip Wylie

Toward the end of the stock market meltdown of 2000–02, some investors became so discouraged that they tossed their monthly statements into the garbage, unread. They simply couldn't bear to see how much money they were losing.

Maybe they thought that imitating an ostrich would help them to sleep better at night. Perhaps it did, for a time. But in the end, such wilful ignorance probably cost them thousands of dollars, money that might have been saved had they paid attention to what was happening and done some damage control.

Occasionally, the blame for such reactions falls on financial advisors who reassure their clients that the worst is over and things are about to take a turn for the better, even as the financial world is crashing around them. But most advisors are pretty good about levelling with their clients. Usually, it is the investor who simply doesn't want to know.

When it comes to investing, ignorance can take many forms,

and sometimes it's hard to draw the line between ignorance and plain stupidity. I've seen plenty of examples of both over the years. Here are three of the most common offences.

Living in fantasyland. I once received an admonition from a reader who accused me of being too harsh in my replies to people who sent in questions that suggested they were totally out of touch with reality. Perhaps he was right—but after being asked for the thousandth time where to invest money for a 10 percent return with no risk, I tend to get a little testy.

When it comes to money, we need to live in the real world. And in that world, there is no such thing as a risk-free 10 percent return—or 8 percent or even 7 percent. There was a time when things were different, but that was many years ago. Back in the early 1980s, when interest rates were very high, you could stick your cash in a money market fund and not worry about anything—except whether the rising rate of inflation would over-take your return. That time may come again, though not if the Bank of Canada can prevent it. Whenever the core inflation rate strays above the target 2 to 3 percent range, the Bank gets very aggressive about pushing rates higher, even if it tips the economy into recession.

Unfortunately, investing reality still eludes many people, such as the gentleman who wrote to ask: "I have $100,000 in an RRSP. Where can I get a rate of return of at least 8 percent on my invest-ment and my investment is guaranteed?" I found myself wonder-ing how he had managed to accumulate that much money in his plan, since he was clearly out of touch with the marketplace. At the time he wrote, the major banks were offering less than 4 percent on 5-year GICs, while 10-year government bonds were yielding less than 5 percent.

One of the basic rules of investing is not to allow expectations to exceed realities. The moment you do, you open yourself up to potential trouble. From time to time, I have been made aware of companies offering very attractive interest rates on what they claim are risk-free investments. The real world doesn't operate that way— no one gives away something for nothing. The higher the quoted return on an investment, the greater the inherent risk. That's an investing axiom you should never forget.

Investing in securities you don't understand. With all the investment choices available these days, I can only shake my head in wonder at how some people insist on putting their money into securities they don't understand. For example, over the past couple of years, I've received repeated requests for information about ways to invest in hedge funds. Hands up now! How many of you really know how a hedge fund works? Hmmm. Nobody. Then let me ask this: If you don't understand the damn things, why are you so anxious to put your money into them?

Most of the people who pour billions of dollars into hedge funds every year know nothing about arbitrage or long/short strategies or leveraging or derivatives trading. They only know that hedge funds are somehow hot and therefore they need to get into them. They haven't a clue about how risky they can be if anything goes wrong.

Well, things do go wrong, sometimes with disastrous consequences. In 1998, Long-Term Capital Management, a hedge fund that had generated huge profits for investors, lost US$4.6 billion in the space of four months, prompting a major financial crisis. Only the direct intervention of then–Federal Reserve Board chairman Alan Greenspan and a Wall Street bailout prevented a total collapse that could have triggered a stock market crash and a recession. Needless to say, investors in the fund lost a bundle.

More recently, in August 2006, Amaranth Advisors LLC, a hedge fund run out of Greenwich, Connecticut, lost 65 percent of its asset value in a single month because of heavy bets on natural gas that didn't pan out. Investors were shocked. They shouldn't have been. We've seen it before, and we will again.

Until now, in Canada, hedge funds have been largely restricted to "sophisticated investors." The term doesn't mean you have to be smart to buy them, only that you need to have a lot of money that you can afford to lose. However, in response to growing demand, the financial community has been working hard to make them available to a wider market—which means you.

One of the ways this is done is through the creation of exchange-traded closed-end funds that invest in hedge funds. An example is the Northwater Market-Neutral Trust, which trades on the Toronto Stock Exchange under the symbol NMN.UN. It provides investors with an opportunity to buy a portfolio of hedge funds that the managers believe, in the words of the 2006 annual report, "have strong expected risk-adjusted returns as well as performance histories that have a low correlation with major equity and debt markets." The report goes on: "In establishing the hedge fund mix, the Investment Advisor seeks out strategies that also have a low correlation with one another, thereby increasing the benefits of diversification and reducing expected volatility."[1]

How much of that did you understand? If your reply is "not much," then hedge funds should not be on your investment shopping list.

Incidentally, back in 2003 when the bull market was starting to gather steam, this fund was trading at over $16 a share. By mid-2007, the price was below $14. You'd have done much better investing in a plain vanilla Canadian stock fund.

Getting in over your head. When it comes to investing, many people seem to want to run before they can walk. This is especially true of younger people who are just sticking their toe in for the first time. They crave action, and dull old mutual funds don't provide it.

Sometimes these folks turn to day trading for their kicks, which to my mind isn't much different than spending the day at a casino. It doesn't take much to set up a day-trading account. But these things can be toxic if you don't really know what you are doing. Talk about a little knowledge being a dangerous thing.

I recently received an email from a 28-year-old man for which the subject line read: "PLEASE HELP ME!!!!" He had made a terrible blunder in his day-trading account, one which may cost him dearly for years to come. He had drafted a letter to the president of the discount brokerage firm with which he was dealing, a subsidiary of a major bank, pleading to be let off the hook. He wanted me to review the letter before he sent it. Here is an abridged version, with the name of the brokerage firm deleted.

> *On April 4, 2007, I placed an order for 7,500 shares of a company called GGL Diamonds Corp. Unfortunately, I entered the wrong share amount as 75,000, which seriously exceeded my net worth. I did not have sufficient funds in my bank account to cover the transaction but the trade was executed immediately.*
>
> *Naturally, I panicked after noticing what I'd just done and when I went to the Intraday Holdings, I noticed that the amount of $89,000 was to come from my bank account. I called the Customer Care Center to try to get this stock sold ASAP but there were no buyers at the time and the stock started to plummet and when I finally sold it, I lost most of my savings.*

I realize that there is a confirmation page but there is also a place where I have to enter my telephone number in case of any problems. I spoke with one of your representatives and she agreed that abnormally large money orders should include a telephone call. I felt abandoned at the end of the day.

In all fairness, how can a corporation that is linked and/or associated with a bank not do more or have the tools on hand to do a background check on a client's net worth or available funds?

Last summer, I lost my job and am currently on EI. For a novice trader like myself, how can you allow me to make such a huge trade? A stock broker whom I spoke with personally said that he wouldn't let his clients with a $3 million net worth execute a trade of this magnitude on a penny stock.

I now realize that one little typographical error can totally ruin someone's life. What I don't understand is why it takes over three business days to check to see whether I have sufficient funds or not. A situation like this, as you can imagine, is totally new and absolutely nauseating to me. I just feel that a big red flag should have been raised when I executed the order. If I'm overdrawn on my bank account, they don't allow me to withdraw funds from the ATM. Shouldn't this be the case with direct investing as well? Mistakes happen and sometimes they can ruin a person's life. I hope you can empathize with how I'm feeling and we can come to some sort of a resolution. I hope to hear from you soon.

What in the world are we to make of this? A 28-year-old man who is collecting employment insurance, trading on-line in penny stocks! This clearly makes no sense. But you also have to ask yourself why the brokerage firm would accept such an account in the first place. Either its standards were far too lax or there was some misrepresentation on the application.

As a footnote to this story, after I replied to this young man, he wrote back as follows: "Can you tell me the best way to get funding for starting a day-trading business or how to get funds for such a project?" All I could do was shake my head in wonder.

There's no doubt that this man lost a lot of sleep over this incident—perhaps he is still doing so. There is no way I could help him after the fact, except by reading his letter and sympathizing with his plight. But his experience may prevent others from a similar fate, if they learn from it.

SLEEP-EASY ADVICE: If you don't understand how a security works, don't invest in it. If you don't have a great deal of investment experience, avoid attempting sophisticated strategies. As a general rule, simpler is better.

Chapter 6

Bubbles

No warning can save a people determined to grow suddenly rich.
—Samuel Jones Loyd (Lord Overstone)

Bubbles are the progeny of the marriage of greed and optimism. They occur whenever a large group of people collectively decide that a particular asset class has suddenly and magically become a source of unlimited wealth. They burst when the folly of such thinking becomes apparent and investors scramble to escape at any price.

Bubbles can indeed create fortunes—but only for those who get in at the beginning and are smart enough to sell when the buying frenzy is at its peak. For most people, bubbles are wealth-destroyers, leaving financial carnage in their wake that can take years to clean up.

Perhaps the most famous manifestation of this phenomenon in history was the South Sea Bubble, which brought England to the brink of financial collapse in the early 18th century. Its beginnings were seemingly innocent. In 1711, Robert Harley, Earl of Oxford, established the South Sea Company. Although we normally think of the South Seas as encompassing the islands of the southern Pacific, the stated purpose of the company was in fact to carry on trade with Mexico and South America—regions which, inconveniently, happened to be under the control of Spain.

"Even at this early period of its history, the most visionary ideas were formed by the company and the public of the immense riches of the western coast of South America," wrote Charles Mackay more than a century later in his classic book *Extraordinary Popular Delusions and the Madness of Crowds*. "Every body had heard of the gold and silver mines of Peru and Mexico; every one believed them to be inexhaustible, and that it was only necessary to send the manufactures of England to the coast, to be repaid a hundredfold in gold and silver ingots by the natives."[1]

So pervasive was the belief that the company would be able to tap into untold wealth that the British Parliament granted the directors a monopoly and later bought into a plan to finance the company in return for what amounted to a promise to pay off the national debt. One of the few voices raised against the scheme in the House of Commons was that of the great parliamentarian Sir Robert Walpole, who was later to become prime minister. Speaking against the measure in 1720, he warned that it would "decoy the unwary to their ruin."

No one paid attention. Walpole was dismissed as an alarmist. The bill passed, and the speculators went crazy. The price of South Sea shares doubled, then doubled again, and again. As Mackay writes, "The public mind was in a state of unwholesome fermentation. Men were no longer satisfied with the slow but sure profits of cautious industry. The hope of boundless wealth for the morrow made them heedless and extravagant for to-day."[2]

The South Sea Company's success spawned many imitators, all designed to relieve gullible people of their wealth. Mackay lists 86 of them in his book, for projects ranging from paving the streets of London to a plan to extract silver from lead. Many of the ventures focused on various forms of insurance, including one to protect "all masters and mistresses [against] the losses they may sustain by servants."[3]

So great was the public desire to participate in these wild schemes, people would buy shares at one end of Exchange Alley (the 18th-century version of a modern stock exchange floor) and sell them for a 10 percent profit a few minutes later at the other end. In the end, of course, the whole house of cards came tumbling down. South Sea Company shares, which at one point traded for as much as £1,000, plunged to zero. Millions were lost, people's lives were ruined, the company directors were disgraced, and parliamentarians scrambled to point the finger of blame elsewhere by launching an inquiry. (That sounds familiar, doesn't it?)

One of those who lost a bundle in the South Sea Bubble was the great scientist Sir Isaac Newton, who turned out to be much more gifted at math than at managing money. Later, he summed up the experience by saying: "I can calculate the motion of heavenly bodies but not the madness of people."

Of course, we're much too sophisticated now to be sucked into another South Sea Bubble, aren't we? Oh yeah? Flash forward more than two centuries to Japan in the 1980s. The country had staged an economic miracle. It had not merely recovered from the ravages of the Second World War; it had thrust itself into a position where it was the world's number two economy, trailing only the United States. The gross domestic product was growing by double digits every year (shades of present-day China). The market value of Japanese companies soared—the benchmark Nikkei Index rose tenfold between 1970 and the beginning of 1990. Cash-rich Japanese conglomerates were buying up iconic U.S. companies such as Columbia Pictures, which Sony purchased in 1989. By one estimate, in 1990, Japanese interests owned 10 percent of America.

Real estate prices in Tokyo staggered the imagination—at one point, the collective property value of the city was said to be worth more than all the land in the United States. American businesspeople flocked to Japan in an effort to learn the secrets of the country's remarkable success. Bestselling books were written about Japan Inc. The Nikkei Index soared to almost 39,000 toward the end of 1989 as investors around the world scrambled to participate in the boom. It was only a matter of time, said some experts, before the country would compete head-to-head with the United States for world economic dominance and Japan would own up to half of Corporate America.

It all turned out to be a magnitude-one bubble. By late 1989, investor confidence in the Nikkei had reached the ultimate optimism stage. That's the point at which profit-takers begin to outnumber new buyers, causing prices to start trending down. In early 1990, the Tokyo Stock Market began to experience what the *International Herald Tribune* would later refer to as "an astonishing collapse." In retrospect, it wasn't so astonishing at all. Valuations had been pushed to such absurd levels that something had to crack, and it did.

The resulting plunge would continue for more than 13 long years, until the Nikkei reached its nadir at a level below 8,000 in the spring of 2003—a decline of about 80 percent. As with the South Sea Bubble, fortunes were lost and lives were ruined. By mid-2007, the index had recovered to the 18,000 level, but that was still more than 50 percent below its 1989 peak. Japanese car makers and electronic manufacturers continue to flourish, but the country is still paying the price for the excesses of the 1980s.

Of course, the primary victims of the bust were the Japanese people themselves. North Americans weren't greatly affected, except to the extent that they had stocked up on Japanese mutual funds. Their turn was to come.

In December 1996, then–Federal Reserve Board chairman Alan Greenspan gave what has been described as a rather dull speech to the American Enterprise Institute, a Washington, D.C., think tank. In it, almost as a throw-away line, he asked, seemingly rhetorically: "How do we know when irrational exuberance has unduly escalated asset values, which then become subject to unexpected and prolonged contractions as they have in Japan over the past decade?"

Although his remarks were made a few years before the dot-com bubble took hold in 1998, they have since been widely interpreted as a warning to avoid the excesses of the internet frenzy. In reality, they were a warning against getting caught up in all bubbles, of whatever form. That dot-com mania exploded a couple of years later was sheer coincidence.

Of course, that's the bubble we all remember, the one that haunts us to this day. At its peak, people were paying ridiculous prices for high-tech companies, just as they did for shares in the South Sea Company almost three hundred years before. For Canadians, Nortel Networks became the symbol of the dot-com collapse. In early 2000, Nortel stock accounted for about a third of the total valuation of the TSX Composite Index and traded for as much as $124.50 a share. Two years later, it had plunged all the way to $0.67. Collectively, we lost billions. Some people have never recovered; they still hold the shares they bought for more than $100 in the forlorn hope the company will one day return to its former glory.[4] It will be a long wait.

Of course, Nortel wasn't the only company to experience a share collapse. Even giants such as Intel and Microsoft saw their stock lose more than half its value. Many smaller firms disappeared entirely. Although all stock market indexes were hit, the plunge of the NASDAQ Composite was the most dramatic. NASDAQ was the incubator for most dot-com stocks, so when the bubble burst, it took by far the worst hit. From early 2000 to the fall of 2002, the index lost close to 80 percent of its value—about the same as the drop in Tokyo's Nikkei Index but in a much shorter time.

Among the heavy losers were Canadian mutual fund investors. The industry flooded the marketplace with technology funds in the late 1990s, and investors, caught up in the greed/optimism syndrome that characterizes bubbles, were quick to snap them up. Many brokers and mutual fund dealers encouraged this speculation, in some cases advising clients to borrow money so they could buy even more of the hot-ticket items, an investing technique known as leveraging. Huge profits in 1999 further fuelled the buying frenzy. During that year, the Altamira e-business Fund, whose mandate was to invest in "companies that are taking advantage of the emerging business opportunities in the digital economy," gained an astounding 190 percent. Money poured in, and by the end of the year total assets stood at $311 million. Unfortunately, the delusions of infinite wealth were short-lived and, as is typical with bubbles, it was the people who joined the party late who paid the heaviest price. Over the next three years, the fund suffered consecutive annual losses of 48 percent, 43 percent, and 41 percent. An investment of $1,000 at the start of 2000 was worth less than $174 at the end of 2003. Investors who held on through those awful years lost almost 83 percent of their money. No wonder so many people were traumatized.[5]

Bubbles aren't confined to stock markets. If they were, you could avoid them by refusing to invest in equities. In fact, they can emerge in any sector of the economy. We've seen bubbles in real estate, in gold, in oil, in sugar, in rare coins, even in tulip bulbs. Indeed, one of the greatest bubbles in history was the infamous tulipomania that swept through Holland in the 17th century. As Mackay wrote, "Substantial merchants were reduced almost to beggary, and many a representative of a noble line saw the fortunes of his house ruined beyond redemption."[6]

The moral of these sad tales for Sleep-Easy investors is simple: Don't let a bubble ruin your financial life. We'll see more of them in the future, and sometimes the lure of easy money and the persuasiveness of the sales pitch can be very tempting. I still recall attending a presentation in North Vancouver in 1999 at which the speaker authoritatively claimed that this time it was different and that stock markets would continue to rise for at least the next decade. In my library, there's a copy of a bestselling book of the day (not one of mine) that extolled readers to get rich by mortgaging their homes to the hilt and investing in mutual funds. Just imagine how the people who took that advice felt around the end of 2002.

SLEEP-EASY ADVICE: Never get swept up in the herd mentality. Eventually, the herd will run off a cliff. Think for yourself, learn to recognize excess when you see it, and stand clear of buying frenzies of whatever type. Despite what the song says, bubbles are not pretty. Never forget that there is nothing inside them but air.

Chapter 7

Weighing Risk

The greater the risk, usually the worse the idea.
—Robert Heller

Last summer, as I was in the process of writing this book, a friend asked me what the title would be. When I told him *Sleep-Easy Investing,* he looked at me incredulously.

"How can you write a whole book on that?" he asked. "It's so easy. Just put all your money into risk-free securities and forget about it."

Too bad it's not that simple. The sad truth is that there is no such thing as a risk-free investment. Not a single one. Every security carries some risk; it's all a matter of degree. The secret to Sleep-Easy investing is deciding the level of risk with which you can live comfortably and adjusting your financial affairs accordingly.

Most people tend to equate risk with speculation. They recognize that there is substantial risk in putting their money into penny stocks and commodity futures. But they see guaranteed investment certificates, government bonds, and even principal-protected notes as being risk-free. That's simply not the case. It's a matter of picking your poison—deciding which risks you can live with and which are unacceptable.

Let's run through the different types of risk you must consider when making financial decisions, some of which may not even have occurred to you.

Inflation Risk

As I write this, the governor of the Bank of Canada is expressing growing concern about the resurgence of inflation and warning that interest rates will likely start rising again soon in an effort to contain it. It's been a long time since we've had to contend with inflation as a major problem, but when it takes hold, the results can be devastating. Many readers will be too young to remember the Trudeau era—from 1968 to the mid-1980s—when inflation became such a serious issue that the federal government imposed wage and price controls. Interest rates soared, savings were ravaged, and the country suffered through one of its most difficult periods since the Second World War.

Hopefully, we won't have to live through that again. But even low-level inflation can pose a serious financial risk if your assets are tied up in investments that offer marginal returns. For example, suppose you have $10,000 that you want to invest in something "safe." A small trust company is offering 5 percent interest on a five-year GIC, paid annually. That's a better rate than the big banks are paying, and it represents $500 worth of income each year. You feel even more comfortable because the investment is protected by deposit insurance. If anything is risk-free, this is it, right?

Well, not really.

Let's suppose the inflation rate when you invest your money is running at 2.2 percent, which is where the Consumer Price Index

(CPI) stood at the time of writing. We'll also assume that the efforts of the Bank of Canada to hold it in check are successful and that the CPI remains unchanged over the next five years. How much money, in real dollars adjusted for inflation, do you think you will actually earn over the five years? Take a look at the table below.

End of Year	Gross Income ($)	Inflation Rate (%)	Real Return (Inflation Adjusted) ($)
1	500	2.2	489.00
2	500	2.2	478.24
3	500	2.2	467.72
4	500	2.2	457.43
5	500	2.2	447.36

As you can see, even at modest rates of inflation, your GIC's before-tax real return falls from 5 percent at the time of purchase to just 4.47 percent at maturity. Plus, the $10,000 you'll get back from the trust company at maturity will have a purchasing power of just $8,947. The money you thought was safely invested has lost 10.5 percent of its real value when you take the impact of inflation into account. And remember, this is at a relatively low rate. Suppose that inflation were to gradually increase over the five-year period, say by two-tenths of a percent annually. Here's what you'd be looking at.

End of Year	Gross Income ($)	Inflation Rate (%)	Real Return (Inflation Adjusted) ($)
1	500	2.2	489.00
2	500	2.4	477.26
3	500	2.6	464.86
4	500	2.8	451.84
5	500	3.0	438.28

In this scenario, the real yield on your original 5 percent investment drops to 4.38 percent by the time the GIC matures, and the buying power of your $10,000 principal has been reduced to $8,766.

Now ask yourself this question: If someone told you in advance that an investment you were considering would lose more than 12 percent of its true value over five years and that the buying power of the income it generated would steadily decline in the process, would you consider that to be a "safe" investment? Probably not. Yet many people persist in believing that GICs are risk-free. They're not—and inflation isn't the only reason.

In fact, inflation is a significant risk with any fixed-income investment, and the longer the term, the greater the risk becomes. At an annual inflation rate of 3 percent, a $50,000 investment will be worth only about $36,900 in terms of real purchasing power after 10 years.

You can protect yourself against inflation risk by putting some of your money into investments that will appreciate in value in line with increases in the cost of living, such as stocks, equity or balanced mutual funds, and real estate. You may have been conditioned to think of these as higher-risk investments, but as I said at the outset of this chapter, it's all a matter of degree. Not to include them in your portfolio will expose you to an unacceptable level of inflation risk.

Tax Risk

It's one thing to invest in interest-bearing securities in a tax-sheltered plan such as an RRSP or RRIF. It's quite another to hold them in a non-registered, taxable portfolio. The Canada Revenue Agency shows no mercy when it comes to interest income—it is taxed at your marginal rate, which for higher-income people could be in excess of 48 percent, depending on the province of residence. Tax risk has reared its ugly head!

With that in mind, let's revisit our original table and see the impact of a marginal tax rate of 30 percent on our real return. Virtually all Canadians with taxable income in excess of $38,000 will pay at least that much.

End of Year	Gross Income ($)	Tax Payable ($)	Nominal After-Tax Income ($)	Inflation (%)	Real Return ($)
1	500	150	350	2.2	342.30
2	500	150	350	2.2	334.77
3	500	150	350	2.2	327.40
4	500	150	350	2.2	320.20
5	500	150	350	2.2	313.16

Not a pretty picture, is it? In terms of buying power, your after-tax, inflation-adjusted return on the GIC in the fifth year is down to a meagre $313.16. That's about 37 percent below the $500 you were counting on when you made the investment. And this is at a low 30 percent marginal rate.

There's another factor to consider. The return on the GIC is locked in for five years, but your tax rate isn't fixed. Hopefully it won't happen, but your marginal rate could conceivably go up during that time, either because you move into a higher bracket or because Ottawa and/or your provincial government decides to increase tax rates to finance environmental programs or daycare, or you move to a province with a higher tax rate.

Tax risk should be a major consideration in your financial planning, and there are several ways to mitigate it, which we'll explore in a subsequent chapter. As a broad guideline, always structure your investment portfolio to take maximum advantage of any legal tax breaks that exist, and be flexible enough to move quickly if the rules change.

Interest Rate Risk

Let's pay a third visit to that $10,000 GIC paying 5 percent. We've looked at how inflation risk and tax risk can erode real returns. As if those aren't enough, there's also interest rate risk to consider.

As I mentioned, at the time of writing, the Bank of Canada was warning that its key interest rate would probably have to rise. We were already seeing the impact of that in the commercial lending market, where mortgage rates were moving higher, and in the bond market, where yields were on the rise.

When a central bank decides that interest rates have to be pushed up to deal with an overheated economy and inflation risk, the governors rarely stop at one increase. Between June 2004 and June 2006, the U.S. Federal Reserve Board raised the federal funds rate 17 consecutive times, all the way from 1 percent to

5.25 percent. So if rates start to rise, you should expect the process to continue for a while, perhaps for a couple of years. Bankers prefer to err on the side of caution where inflation is concerned.

If that should happen, financial institutions would move in lockstep by raising borrowing rates and GIC yields accordingly. So by the time your GIC is into its third year, five-year rates could be in the 6 to 7 percent range. That's a lot better than your GIC is paying now, but you're stuck. Because most GICs are locked in until maturity, you have no choice but to wait it out and hope you can secure a better rate at that time. Of course, interest rates may have declined again by then, and the opportunity for a higher return will have vanished. You've just encountered one version of interest rate risk.

But at least you can cash in a GIC for its face value at maturity. If you were holding conventional bonds, traded on the bond market, a rise in interest rates will produce a drop in the value of your securities. You won't even be able to get your principal back if you want to sell. You could wait until the bonds mature, of course. But that may not be for 15 or 20 years.

A second type of interest rate risk occurs when interest rates drop dramatically and high-yielding GICs have to be rolled over at lower rates. We saw an example of that at the beginning of this century. Worried by a strong economy and stock market excesses, the Federal Open Market Committee of the U.S. Federal Reserve Board ratcheted interest rates higher in the late 1990s and into 2000. By May 2000, the federal funds rate was at 6.5 percent, its highest level in years. In a statement issued at the time, the Fed said: "Increases in demand have remained in excess of even the rapid pace of productivity-driven gains in potential supply, exerting continued pressure on resources. The Committee is concerned that this disparity in the growth of demand and potential supply will continue, which could foster inflationary imbalances that would undermine the economy's outstanding performance."

The Canadian pattern was similar. The Bank of Canada moved its key rate from 4.75 percent in the fall of 1999 all the way to 6 percent by the end of 2000, for much the same reasons as the Federal Reserve Board. The average interest rate on five-year chartered bank GICs moved right along, rising as high as 5.73 percent in 2000. Then the reality of the stock market crash and the corresponding economic slowdown began to bite. The bank rate fell all the way to 2.25 percent in the winter of 2003. GIC rates were slower to react, but by the middle of 2003 the banks were offering only 2.8 percent on five-year money. Even that wasn't the low point. When new concerns about the economy surfaced in 2004, the bank rate dropped again, falling to as low as 2.25 percent in the spring. This time the commercial banks didn't lag behind; in March 2004, the average five-year GIC rate was down to 2.38 percent.

The impact was devastating for GIC investors whose certificates matured at that time. Five years earlier, in March 1999, they had received a yield of 4.48 percent. Now their GICs were being rolled over at a rate that was 47 percent less. To put that in perspective, anyone who invested $10,000 in a five-year GIC in March 1999 would have received annual interest of $448. In March 2004, that was reduced to $238. It was the equivalent of an employee being told his or her salary would be cut in half.

Interest rate risk needs to be taken into account with every type of fixed-income investment. The best way to minimize it is to hold some securities that are easily convertible into cash, such as money market funds, bankers' acceptances, and Treasury bills. If interest rates begin to move up, you can quickly switch your money into other investments that will maximize your short-term returns while keeping you flexible enough to make longer-range commitments when appropriate.

Stock Market Risk

Nobody needs to be reminded that the stock market can be a risky place—not after the horrendous losses of 2000–02. Every market in the world was affected, though none took a bigger hit than the technology-heavy NASDAQ exchange, which shed about 80 percent of its value during the period.

Stock market risk is a constant fact of life for equity investors. And, like most other forms of risk, it is unpredictable. Few people expected the high-tech sector to suddenly start melting down in the early spring of 2000, eventually dragging down the rest of the stock market with it. But it happened.

It you invest in equities (and that includes equity mutual funds), stock market risk is a fact of life. However, you can minimize the risk in three ways: by buying only top-quality stocks, by having a time horizon that's long enough to enable you to ride out any temporary setbacks, and by diversifying your portfolio. I'll have more to say about this in Chapter 16.

Political Risk

We don't have to look any farther for a classic example of political risk than to the announcement made by Conservative Finance Minister Jim Flaherty on Halloween night, 2006. Under the guise of a Tax Fairness Plan, the minister pulled the rug from under Canada's booming income trust industry and in the process cost investors, many of them retirees, billions of dollars.

Supporters of the government said the investors should have seen it coming. That's nonsense. In announcing a 31.5 percent tax on income trust distributions to take effect in 2011, the finance minister broke a written Conservative Party campaign promise that

no action would be taken against the trusts. People had taken the
Tories at their word, only to find less than a year after voting them
into office that the pledge was worthless. (I discuss this in more
detail in Chapter 12.)

Niccolò Machiavelli wrote: "Put not your trust in princes,
bureaucrats, or generals, they will plead experience while spilling
your blood from a safe distance." That's exactly what Mr. Flaherty
did—he spilled the financial blood of hundreds of thousands of
Canadians while pleading the expediency of taxation necessity.
With BCE, Telus, and EnCana about to convert from corporate to
trust status, Ottawa faced the loss of millions of corporate tax
dollars, the country was told. Interestingly, to this day the Finance
Department has never produced credible numbers to back up that
assertion.

The finance minister later said that he was sorry about the more
than $30 billion in market capitalization that was wiped out (some
of which was later recovered as trusts rallied in 2007), but that it
just couldn't be helped. The rush to trusts simply had to be
stopped.

As usual, it was ordinary people who paid the price. One British
Columbia railroad worker wrote to me as follows:

> I just reached my forty-ninth birthday last week, working for
> the past 30 years on BC Rail. I have an RRSP that as of
> October 30 had a balance of $53,000. Within a couple of
> days, I watched it dwindle to about $38,000. I feel let down
> by my own government.

As well he should. I received many, many emails that told much
the same story. People were blindsided and many, in panic, sold
their trust units into a tumbling market, taking big losses in the

process. In a single statement, Canada's leaders destroyed billions in personal wealth and reminded us, once again, why we should never put our trust in princes or bureaucrats—or politicians.

Default Risk

The concept of default risk is very simple: You buy a security, the issuer declares bankruptcy, and you're left with little or nothing. It can happen with almost any type of investment: bonds, common stocks, preferred shares, hedge fund units, and so on.

According to a study by David T. Hamilton and Sharon Ou published in the summer 2004 issue of the *Canadian Investment Review,* between 1989 and 2003, a total of 61 Canadian companies defaulted on bonds worth a total of $31 billion. These weren't all small firms; in fact, the largest defaulter was AT&T Canada, which stiffed its bondholders for $4.6 billion in September of 2002. Although most of the defaults involved bonds rated as "speculative," the authors found some that were rated as high as Baa by Moody's, an international bond-rating agency.

Bond defaults are more prevalent during economic downturns, when high-debt companies find they are overextended. During periods of strong economic growth, they are much rarer—Moody's reported that, in 2002, defaults in Canada exceeded $14 billion but, in 2005 and 2006, when the economy was surging, they fell to zero.

Stock market defaults, on the other hand, can happen any time. A recent example is FMF Capital, a Delaware-incorporated company that was headquartered in Southfield, Michigan, with branch offices in Nashville, Tennessee, and Virginia Beach, Virginia. While the company was active, it operated in 39 U.S. states, using a network of 4,400 mortgage brokers.

FMF was sold under prospectus in Canada in early 2005 as an Income Participating Security (IPS)—similar in concept to an income trust in cash flow terms but with a corporate structure. The company was involved in residential mortgage lending in the United States, primarily in the troubled subprime market. It would originate mortgage loans for people who could not qualify through the banking system because of poor credit and then resell the loans to institutional purchasers within an average of 39 days of funding. The U.S. subprime market took a severe beating in late 2006 and into 2007, to the point where it threatened to drag down the major stock indexes with it. However, FMF's troubles dated back almost to the time it went public in Canada.

When FMF was brought to market, it was promoted by a Michigan firm, Michigan Fidelity Acceptance Corporation (MFAC). The final prospectus covering the terms of the offering contains these legal references to the companies:

> It may not be possible for investors to collect from MFAC judgments obtained in Canada predicated on the civil liability provisions of securities legislation of certain of the provinces and territories of Canada. There can be no assurance of recovery by an IPS holder from MFAC for judgments obtained in courts in Canada predicated on the civil liability provisions of securities legislation of certain of the provinces and territories of Canada, or (ii) the Issuer from MFAC for any breach of the representations and warranties provided by MFAC under the Acquisition Agreement, as there can be no assurance that the assets of MFAC will be sufficient to satisfy any such liability or contractual obligations set out in the Acquisition Agreement.[1]

In other words: Buyer beware.

FMF's IPO price was $10 a share, and the company sought to raise almost $200 million. The shares began trading in spring 2005 and almost immediately fell below the offering price. FMF was trading at $4.72 when the company announced the suspension of distributions in November 2005. Predictably, the shares plunged, falling to $1.73, a loss of 77 percent. They continued to drift lower after that. On March 6, 2007, the Toronto Stock Exchange announced that trading in FMF units was suspended pending delisting. At the time, the shares were trading at $0.06. Three days later, FMF announced it was winding up its business, saying in a statement: "This decision by the Company was made as a result of the continuing rapid and severe deterioration of the U.S. nonprime mortgage industry and other factors affecting its overall nonprime mortgage business." The move came after FMF reported a third-quarter (October to December 2006) loss of US$23.6 million, which included a US$22.6 million writeoff of intangible assets and goodwill.

On April 4, 2007, the TSX delivered the coup de grâce, officially delisting FMF. The default process was complete, and original shareholders who had held on until the end lost everything.

Yes, there were warnings this might happen. The offering prospectus contained about a dozen pages of risk notices. However, they were buried deep within the document (starting at page 122), and many were the boilerplate kind of stuff that you'd read in any prospectus. Few investors would have looked at them, instead relying on guidance from their advisors or the reputation of the underwriters.

And who were the underwriters that brought this company to the Canadian market? The group was led by BMO Nesbitt Burns, which owns the trademark for the term "Income Participating

Security." Other participants, as listed in the prospectus, were National Bank Financial, TD Securities, Canaccord Capital Corporation, First Associates Investments, and Sprott Securities. As far as I can determine, none of them ever had anything to say about the debacle that ensued.

The best way to minimize default risk is to do some homework. There are a number of services in Canada and the United States that rate various types of securities, such as bonds, income trusts, and preferred shares and their ratings, with commentaries, and that are available on the internet for everyone to view. Standard & Poor's Canada, Dominion Bond Rating Service, and Moody's are among the best. To protect yourself against default risk, never buy a bond with a rating of less than A (AAA is the top level), or a preferred share with a rating of less than P-2. When it comes to stocks, do thorough research unless you are buying shares in a large, well-known company.

Economic Risk

Economic risk can occur in a variety of forms: a jump in the inflation rate that causes bond prices to drop, a bumper harvest that knocks down grain prices, a slowdown in consumer spending that leads to a drop in car and house sales, a drop in natural gas prices that causes the share price of producer companies to fall, a rise in the Canadian dollar that hits the profits of exporters—all of these have negative implications for investors.

Economic risk can be triggered by mega-events, such as the 9/11 attacks. Or it can involve a specific industry, as we saw with the high-tech collapse. The best way to mitigate this risk is to be vigilant about what's going on in the world and understand how economic news may affect your investments.

Liquidity Risk

I have a copy of the first edition of a book titled *V,* by the novelist Thomas Pynchon. One day I read in a magazine that this edition was worth over $300. Terrific, I thought. I'm not a collector of first editions. I didn't particularly care for the book. It was just gathering dust on a shelf. Why not convert it to cash?

It seemed like a good idea, but trying to find a buyer who would pay $300 for it was impossible. I visited several rare book stores along Toronto's Queen Street West. The best offer I got was $100. I still have the damn book.

That's liquidity risk. You may have an asset that's worth a lot of money, but it's no good unless someone is prepared to pay your price for it. If you can't sell it for what it's supposedly worth, you've got a problem.

It's a risk that crops up more often than you might expect. For example, some people have invested in thinly traded penny stocks only to find there were no buyers when the time came to sell. I know of investors who bought condos in Toronto hoping to make a quick profit who were left having to pay stiff financing costs because they couldn't sell into an overbuilt market. Each winter when I'm in Florida I see the same houses with For Sale signs— they've been sitting on the front lawn for two or three years. The owners obviously want to get their money out but can't because there's a surfeit of residential property on the market.

Liquidity risk can be reduced by ensuring that anything you invest in has a strong and ready market of potential buyers. If it doesn't, find someplace else for your money.

By now you may be wondering whether it's worth investing in anything. With all that risk out there, you may be tempted to bury your money in the backyard. Actually, it's not that bad. The list seems daunting, but you can make money by investing and, in keeping with the theme of this book, sleep well in the process. The important thing is to recognize from the outset that there are risks and then to weigh your investment decisions accordingly.

This is where something called the risk/return ratio comes into play. Simply put, it means that the greater the risk you're taking, the higher the potential return on your investment should be.

That's why commodities futures—high risk—offer a much greater potential reward than Treasury bills—low risk.

Here's a typical risk/return ladder, with low-risk investments at the bottom:

High Risk

Commodity Futures
Currencies
Hedge funds
Options and warrants
Gold and precious metals
Common stocks
Equity mutual funds
Preferred shares
Bonds
Guaranteed investment certificates
Canada savings bonds
Money market funds
Bankers' acceptances
Treasury bills
Deposit accounts

Low Risk

Use this list as a guideline only, since it's a simplified version. For example, there are some bonds that are more risky than blue chip common stocks, with a lower potential return.

As a general rule, lower-risk securities have less profit potential but offer a higher degree of safety. The challenge is to weigh the relative risk/return of any investment you're considering and to decide if it fits into your master plan. When making those decisions, take these six factors into account.

Age. The younger you are, the more risk you can build into your investment portfolio. That's because you have many years to recoup your losses (although you'll be better off if you can avoid them entirely). Even if you invested a lot of money in the stock market in early 2000, there's a good chance you would have recovered all your losses by mid-2007 and have some nice profits.

But older baby boomers and retirees don't have time on their side. That's why the older you are, the more you have to favour safety over profit if you are going to have a true Sleep-Easy portfolio.

Family situation. The greater your family obligations, the less risk you can afford to assume. If you have dependants—young children, aged parents, or a disabled spouse—you must be far more cautious in your investing approach than if you're single and carefree. But even people with heavy family responsibilities are sometimes tempted to take higher than normal risks in the hope of a big payoff that will ease their ongoing financial burden. It's not a great idea.

Security. Preservation of capital should be the primary goal of every Sleep-Easy investment portfolio. If you lose a big chunk of your principal, it will take years to recover financially, and you may never recover emotionally.

Income needs. If you are counting on your investments to generate income, you'll want to concentrate your portfolio in securities that pay a predictable return at specified intervals. We'll look at some of those further on in the book, in Chapter 16.

Growth. A high-growth portfolio will be constructed quite differently from one that emphasizes income. Usually, it will involve a higher degree of risk—although there are ways of mitigating this, as we'll see later.

Diversification. Any Sleep-Easy investment portfolio must be well diversified, not just in terms of the number of securities held but also in the type of assets. This is more complicated than simply deciding how much to invest in stocks and how much in bonds, and I'll provide details in Chapter 16.

> **SLEEP-EASY ADVICE:** Each risk factor is relevant; don't lose sight of any of them. The key to success is to create a proper risk/return balance that meets your specific needs.

Chapter 8

Hot Tip Nightmares

Bulls and bears aren't responsible for as many stock losses as bum steers.
—Olin Miller

Suppose a good friend came up to you at a party and pulled you aside. "You've got to keep this quiet," he whispers when you're out of earshot of everyone. "I just heard this from one of the directors of Big Wind Corporation and it hasn't been announced yet. It's received a takeover bid from the Mighty Gale Company in the United States, and the board has voted to approve it. The offer is for double its stock's trading price. I told my broker today to buy me a thousand shares. You should do the same thing before the news gets out."

Ask yourself honestly: What would you do in this situation?

a. Thank your friend for the tip and call your broker first thing in the morning.
b. Thank your friend for the tip and ignore it.
c. Tell your friend that what he's done could get him arrested and that you won't have any part of it.

The correct response is, of course, the third one. Your friend has received confidential information from a company insider and has acted on it for his personal benefit. That's illegal, and though people sometimes get away with it, especially if they are not a director or officer of the company, anyone who tries to profit from such privileged information is taking a big risk. If you chose option a and called your broker to place an order for Big Wind shares, you'd be in the same situation.

The reality, however, is that many people would take the risk, sometimes because they don't know the rules, and sometimes using the rationale that because they "heard it from a friend who heard it from a friend," they aren't doing anything unlawful and, anyway, no one is going to be hurt because you bought a few shares. It's easy to justify immoral behaviour when there's a lot of money on the table.

The fact that insider trading is illegal should be a compelling reason not to act on tips like this. But if that's not enough to persuade you, try this: Nine times out of ten, you'll lose money by betting on hot tips. Why? Because by the time you hear about it, hundreds or perhaps thousands of other people will already be in on the story and will have placed orders for the stock, driving the price higher. As a result, you overpay.

Why would a company director do something like that, you may ask? Let's construct a hypothetical scenario. Suppose this particular director holds a large number of shares in Big Wind. He has just come through a messy divorce and is faced with a huge settlement plus legal bills. He is short of cash and needs to get his hands on some quickly.

As a director, he knows that Big Wind is having serious problems. A strike at the European plant that manufactures turbines for the company has put construction of the new wind farm on the east shore of Hudson Bay at least six months behind schedule. Without the revenue from the electricity production that had been budgeted, the company faces a serious cash crunch within a few months. The share price has already started to fall as a result.

The director is desperate. He must sell stock to raise the money he needs, but the price is depressed. So he begins a surreptitious rumour campaign, telling a few people that he knows are chronically incapable of discretion that Big Wind is about to be taken over. It works exactly as he expects. The word spreads, the stock moves sharply higher, and he is able to sell his shares at a fat profit—more than enough to pay off his ex-wife and the lawyers, with plenty left over for a vacation in Hawaii.

Meantime, when the stock exchange sees what is happening to the share price, it asks the chief executive officer of Big Wind for an explanation. A few days later, the company issues a press release stating that rumours of a takeover bid are completely unfounded and no talks are active or contemplated with Mighty Gale or anyone else. The stock price immediately plunges as panicky investors, some of whom borrowed heavily to buy shares, try to unload. And who's left holding the bag? The poor suckers who believed the hot tip and bought a couple of hundred shares with the expectation of cashing in on a sure thing.

Farfetched? Hardly. Variations of this scenario happen all the time, and there are always easy marks out there to prey on.

When it comes to the stock market, the "get rich quick" syndrome is hard to cure. Investors are always looking for the "big score," that one stock that will make them fabulously wealthy overnight. It appears to be as addictive as gambling.

The reality is that it rarely happens that way. You stand a much better chance of making a big score by buying a blue chip stock when it's cheap and being patient than you do by chasing hot tips.

For example, in April 1997, I advised readers of my *Internet Wealth Builder* newsletter to buy shares of what was then Brascan Corporation, a huge Toronto-based conglomerate with interests in everything from real estate to power generation. A decade later, those who followed that guidance were sitting on a capital gain of 575 percent and were receiving a dividend yield of 9.1 percent, based on their original purchase price.[1]

But 10 years is too long for many people to wait, especially in this era of instant gratification. They don't want to be patient, they want it now! So the hot tip industry continues to flourish.

Not that it has ever languished in this country. Canada has a long and dubious history of stock promotion. In years past, the now-defunct Vancouver Stock Exchange (VSE) had a well-deserved reputation of being a financial Wild West. Professional tipsters earned big bucks by talking up obscure mining ventures to raise equity. Since casinos weren't legal in this country at the time, the VSE was the next best thing.

One of the most famous of these promoters was David Walsh, who eventually became CEO of the company that is synonymous with stock fraud in Canada, Bre-X Minerals. Several books have been written about the Bre-X saga, so I am not going to rehash the story here. I only cite it because it is the ultimate example of the damage hot tips can do. In this case, even seasoned professionals were taken in by the massive con, with brokers advising their clients to take a position in the company's "can't miss" mine in Indonesia, said to be the richest gold strike in the history of the world. Bre-X went from being a penny stock to costing more than $200 a share before the scam was revealed. To this day, no one has ever been convicted of any crime, despite the losses of billions of dollars suffered by investors. David Walsh died in 1998 at the age of 52 before he could be brought to trial on charges.

Today, the image of the stock promoter working the investment trade shows seems like ancient history. Hot tips have gone high-tech, and the internet has become the new playground of the stock touts. A large percentage of the billions of spam messages that flash through cyberspace daily are promotions for dubious stocks of all types. Let me pause here for just a moment to plow through my junk email folder and see what's supposedly hot today.

Here's one: Score One Inc. It trades on the over-the-counter (OTC) Pink Sheets in the United States, as do many of the securities that are promoted in this way. The trading symbol is SREA. The email says: "Up another 20% today and over 272% in the last 7 days, OTCPICKS.com puts SREA on their watch list. Read up and get on SREA first thing Wed!"

Checking out the stock on the Pink Sheets website, I saw that it was up 46 percent on the day I received the email (a Wednesday) on a large volume of 572,000 shares. It appeared the hot tip spam was doing its job. The buying frenzy continued on Thursday as the impact of the spam continued, with the price pushing all the way to US$0.69. And then the expected happened. The stock opened at US$0.60 on Friday and proceeded to plummet from there as investors scrambled desperately to bail out. By the time it was all over, another 529,000 shares had changed hands and the stock was all the way back down to US$0.30—a harrowing drop of 56 percent from the high it had touched just the day before. The folks who bought in on the strength of the hot tip email were being whipsawed.

I then went to a website called spamnation.com, where I saw that the spam promotion had already been running for seven days, with a total of 216 messages received promoting the stock. I did a Google search for the company's website. Apparently, there isn't one, but I found a press release that told me it is a Hong Kong–based investment firm that is involved in the development of something called "Recreation Town" near the city of Dalian in northern China. I could not find any financial reports for the company, and a search of the U.S. Securities and Exchange Commission website came up blank. I then looked at the stock's chart on Yahoo! Finance, which showed me that the shares were trading around US$0.15 the previous week, moved all the way to US$0.40 a couple of days later, fall back, then soared again, and were now retreating.

A few weeks later, I revisited the stock. It was no longer being quoted on the Pink Sheets. Instead, there was a message saying: "Pink Sheets has received complaints regarding faxes and/or emails sent in promotion of this stock that may violate federal law. Pink Sheets does not send out or authorize any kind of soliciting email or faxes to the public."

I felt a brief pang of sympathy for the people who had bought shares on the basis of the hot tip spam they had received, but it quickly passed. Anyone stupid enough to purchase a stock as a result of a spam tip deserves what they get.

Now it may be that Score One Inc. is a perfectly legitimate operation. The point is that I don't have enough information to know one way or the other, and presumably neither did the folks who were feverishly buying the shares. As far as I could tell, the only motivation for the activity was email.

These spam messages can take many forms. Some are so crude that you have to wonder how anyone can take them seriously. Others purport to be private email exchanges that you have somehow been copied on. Still others appear at first glance to be legitimate investment newsletters, until you read the fine print. There you discover that the glowing stock reviews they contain are in fact paid advertisements.

One such example I found through a Google search is called the *Superstar Stock Letter*. I called up an issue dated November 10, 2004, in which the email publication focused on shares in a company called e-Food Safety Com Inc. The contents amounted to nothing more than a series of press releases and quotes from a publication called *The KonLin Letter*, which had set a short-term target price of US$2 on the stock. At the bottom, in a lengthy disclaimer, people could read:

This publication is an independent publication with the goal of giving investors the necessary knowledge to make rational and profitable investment decisions.

That makes it sound legit, right? See what you think after reading these excerpts from what follows.

This publication does not provide an analysis of the Companys [sic] financial position…. This is not purported to be a complete and thorough analysis of the featured company…. The publisher discloses the receipt of six thousand dollars from a third party, not an officer, director, or affiliate shareholder of the company for the preparation of this online report.

Be aware of an inherent conflict of interest resulting from such compensation due to the fact that this is a paid publication."[2]

Aha! Someone—we aren't told who—paid the Broadcast Group of Savannah, Georgia, $6,000 to prepare and distribute this report. Now how much confidence do you have in its contents?

For the record, in late June 2007, shares of e-Food Safety were trading at US$0.30. They never got anywhere near the "short-term target" of US$2.00.

By one estimate, Americans and Canadians receive more than one hundred million hot tip spam messages every week. If anything, that's an underestimate; sometimes it seems as though I have that many in my own junk email folder. Most people wisely ignore them, but it appears that enough get hooked to encourage the spammers to keep doing it. The situation has become so serious that the Ontario Securities Commission has posted a warning on its website which states in part:

> A person sending a spam message may have bought stock previously and wants to make a profit by sending the price higher. Spam messages often make it appear that the sender has information that a pending announcement will boost the price of a stock, or that the sender is an independent analyst who views the stock favourably and is setting a high target price. The spammer may also short the stock (borrow stock to sell at a high price, hoping it will drop, and buy it back at the lower price to make a profit) and attempt to lower the price by posting negative information or issuing a negative analysis.
>
> Spammers try to capitalize on your willingness to act without having verified the validity information or analysis. When the price of a security rises on this type of speculation, market forces soon return the price back to realistic levels. When this happens, people who acted without properly researching the investment stand to lose some or all of their investment.
>
> Be wary of opportunities that promise low or no risk, spectacular profits or guaranteed returns. No investment is

risk free and sometimes the investment products touted do not even exist—they are scams.

If you receive an unsolicited message offering investment advice, ask yourself why you received the message and why the person who sent it is trying to remain anonymous by failing to include a legitimate name and contact information. Do your own research and be wary of acting on rumours.[3]

The Securities Commission also has a warning about trading stocks over-the-counter on the Pink Sheets and the OTC Bulletin Board (OTCBB) in which it advises investors to be cautious. "Companies listed on the OTCBB must file financial reports with the United States Securities and Exchange Commission (SEC), but do not have to meet the listing requirements of the major exchanges," the OSC points out. "The Pink Sheets are listings of price quotes for companies that trade in the OTC market. The Pink Sheets are not regulated by Canadian securities regulators or the SEC."[4]

Numerous other websites contain specific alerts about investment spam emails, including the previously mentioned spamnation.com—which, unfortunately, also uses annoying pop-up ads to get your attention. One of the most interesting is stockspamtracker.com, where Joshua Cyr, who is chief technology officer for a software company, displays a list of spam-promoted companies that he tracked over the course of several months in 2005–06 and shows what would have happened had he invested in each at the time. Of the 105 stocks, all but three ended up losing money, and in many cases the loss was 100 percent.

Another source of hot stock tips is online bulletin boards where investors share ideas. The U.S. Securities and Exchange Commission (SEC) has issued a warning that in some cases the boards are being manipulated by unscrupulous promoters:

Online bulletin boards—whether newsgroups, usenet, or web-based bulletin boards—have become an increasingly popular forum for investors to share information. Bulletin boards typically feature "threads" made up of numerous messages on various investment opportunities.

While some messages may be true, many turn out to be bogus—or even scams. Fraudsters often pump up a company or pretend to reveal "inside" information about upcoming announcements, new products, or lucrative contracts.

Also, you never know for certain who you're dealing with—or whether they're credible—because many bulletin boards allow users to hide their identity behind multiple aliases. People claiming to be unbiased observers who've carefully researched the company may actually be company insiders, large shareholders, or paid promoters. A single person can easily create the illusion of widespread interest in a small, thinly-traded stock by posting a series of messages under various aliases.[5]

One common tactic is called "pump and dump." The SEC describes it this way:

They may be insiders or paid promoters who stand to gain by selling their shares after the stock price is pumped up by gullible investors. Once these fraudsters sell their shares and stop hyping the stock, the price typically falls and investors lose their money. Fraudsters frequently use this ploy with small, thinly-traded companies because it's easier to manipulate a stock when there's little or no information available about the company.[6]

Thus far, all efforts by governments, securities regulators, and the technology industry to halt stock shilling on the internet has had little effect. The old "there's a sucker born every minute" cliché is still alive and well, and as long as spam campaigns succeed in pushing up penny stock prices, they'll continue.

SLEEP-EASY ADVICE: If you fall for a scam, it will be a long time before you sleep easy again. There is only one thing to do with a hot tip, regardless of the source: Delete it from your computer and from your mind.

Chapter 9

Get Rich—Go into Debt!

Leverage was the beverage
That got this party cookin'
But the hangover's set in,
And now a Gravedancer's lookin'
—Sam Zell

If I told you there is a way to double your investment returns while getting a big tax break at the same time, would you be interested? Many people would be—in fact, bestselling books have been written on precisely that theme. Not by me, however. Nor will there ever be one.

This strategy, which is known as leveraging, involves borrowing money, often against the equity in your home, to buy stocks or mutual funds. Under Canadian law, the interest paid on the loan becomes tax deductible because the money has been used for investing.

I see leveraging as the financial equivalent of a loaded gun. People who are knowledgeable can use it effectively; everyone else will probably shoot themselves in the foot.

In the first chapter, I told you about a couple who had ended up in deep doo-doo by succumbing to the temptation to borrow big-time in an effort to get rich quick. Here is exactly what happened, as described by the wife in an email that I received in summer 2006.

> *My husband and I are both 62 and still working. Because we had little put away for retirement our financial adviser persuaded us to take out $300,000 in leveraged loans for a seven-year period. This was in April 2006. As at the end of June, the mutual funds have already decreased from $300,000 to $290,000. I am terrified of losing everything and want to sell but my husband wants to hold on. We do not have many years to recover. If we sold now we have a loss of $10,000 plus the service charges of 5.5% will cost another $16,500 for a total loss of $26,500. Is it better to take the loss now before the market sinks any further?*

This woman's obvious fear underlines the main objection I have always had to the use of leveraging by unsophisticated investors. The math may be compelling but emotion will probably trump rationality if push comes to shove.

Let's dissect what happened here, reading between the lines in some cases. This couple is apparently relatively well-off—they would have to be in order to qualify for $300,000 in loans. But they hadn't put much aside for retirement and were starting to worry about how they would cope when they both stop working in a few years, since it appears they don't have pension plans. So they went to their financial advisor for help.

He looked at the situation and found that a large percentage of their net worth was tied up in the equity in their home. As many advisors have done in recent years, he suggested using that idle equity to increase their net worth. This could be done by taking out a home equity line of credit, with an interest rate that was probably one-quarter percent over prime. The real cost would be less because the interest charges would be deductible. The plan was to invest the money for seven years. The math he presented to them to make the case may have looked something like this:

Investing $300,000 for seven years at an average annual compound rate of return of 10 percent results in a portfolio valued at about $585,000 at the end of the period. After the loan is repaid, the couple is left with $285,000. Assuming an average interest rate of 6 percent and a marginal tax rate of 40 percent, the net cost of carrying the loan is $10,800 a year or $75,600 over the seven years. When all is said and done, the couple comes out ahead by around $210,000, which is invested in income-generating securities to help fund their retirement.

At a time when stock markets were in a bull phase and mutual funds were posting healthy gains, it must have seemed like a compelling argument. And it might eventually work out just as the advisor planned—if the wife was able to overcome her anxieties.

What happened was that shortly after the plan was put into place, the stock markets experienced a correction. That's why the portfolio valuation dropped $10,000 between the beginning of April and the end of June. At that point, the wife and the husband were at odds over what to do. She was desperate to get out, even at the cost of another $16,500 which suggests the funds were bought on a deferred sales charge (DSC) basis. (The 5.5 percent is the commission that would be charged for selling early.) "I am terrified of losing everything," she writes. Her husband, however, wanted to stay the course. Can't you see the arguments, the tears, the anguish? Not pretty.

As it turned out, staying the course would have been the right approach, at least at that stage. The markets recovered and stocks went on to record big gains over the next twelve months. With the major North American indexes (except NASDAQ) reaching historic highs in the first half of 2007, July 2006 would definitely not have been the time to bail out. Who can predict what will happen before the seven years are over, however? If we experience another bear market of the kind we lived through between 2000 and 2002, the whole project could end in financial disaster and their retirement prospects would be grimmer than ever.

My advice to this lady was to have a frank heart-to-heart discussion with the advisor about the situation, and to review the entire portfolio carefully with him. If appropriate, they could restructure the investments in a way that minimized risk and was more defensive. For example, they could choose some conservatively managed mutual funds with a track record of having performed well in the 2000–02 bear market.

I hope she took that advice and didn't give in to her panic. If you are going to use leveraging, you must be prepared to stick with the plan for the long haul and not allow emotions to get in the way. If that is psychologically difficult for you, then don't go down that road.

Some financial advisors aggressively encourage clients to use leveraging because of the significant fees and commissions they can earn. Consider the $300,000 our couple borrowed to invest in mutual funds. Since the units were apparently purchased on a DSC basis, the advisor immediately earned a sales commission from the fund company, typically 5 percent. That's an instant payment of $15,000. On top of that, he'll receive a "trailer fee" of perhaps 1 percent annually for as long as the couple owns their fund units. On a $300,000 portfolio, that's worth $3,000 a year.

Plus, he may get a referral fee from the financial services company that underwrote the loan. It all adds up to a nice piece of change.

Advisors can be especially persuasive during bull markets, when stock prices are soaring and everyone seems to be making money. That's when greed takes over and fear recedes into the background. We saw a classic example of that during the technology bubble of the late 1990s. The price of popular tech stocks rose to unheard-of levels and science and technology mutual funds posted huge gains. At the same time, housing prices were rising and home equity lines of credit were gaining widespread acceptance as a quick and convenient source of cash. It was profitable convergence for leverage-happy advisors and a perfect storm for unwary investors.

In fairness, many advisors steered their clients toward lower-risk securities. But a few overloaded the leveraged portfolios with high-tech stocks and mutual funds. As we saw in an earlier chapter, the NASDAQ Composite Index fell about 80 percent between 2000 and 2002. People who had invested aggressively lost virtually everything.

You would think that in this kind of situation, an investor could sue the advisor to recover at least part of the loss. Not so, said the Ontario Superior Court of Justice in a ruling handed down in December 2005.[1] The case had been brought against several financial institutions by 22 elderly investors who had suffered heavy losses as a result of leveraged investments in mutual funds made in the late 1990s. They alleged that the institutions and their advisors made "negligent misrepresentations" and that they "failed to carry out properly their fiduciary duty and their duty of care to the plaintiffs to advise them properly about their loans."

In its ruling, the Court said that "in the late 1990s each of the plaintiffs wished to supplement their resources by investment but they had very limited funds available for that purpose." They therefore contacted financial advisors (two in particular were named) to arrange for investment loans, which were subsequently put in place.

The Court neatly summarized the situation by saying:

> Where a person invests money that he or she already has, the investor obtains a chance of gain if the value of the investment increases and takes a risk of loss if the value of the investment decreases (the 'investment risk'). Where the investor instead borrows funds in order to invest, the investor takes a risk that is additional to the investment risk. This is the risk that if the investment decreases in value, the investor will not be able to rely solely on the value of the investment to repay the loan and thus may be obliged to use other resources to repay the loan (the 'loan risk'). In such circumstances, the investor can end up, not only without an investment of value, but also with an unsatisfied repayment liability to the lender which could be a burdensome obligation.

A "burdensome obligation" was exactly what the investors in this case were left with after the market crash. They wanted the financial institutions and the brokers involved to repay them on the grounds they were badly advised. They claimed they had not read the various documents they had signed because "no one told them to." They told the Court the financial institutions had failed in their fiduciary duty to advise them of the terms and the risks.

The case was thrown out in a summary judgment before it could ever go to trial. The Court concluded "there are no genuine issues of fact for trial" and that the legal issues all favoured the defendants. "It is the borrower who decides to take the loan and so creates whatever foreseeable risk may thereby arise," the Court ruled.

Subsequently, in 2007 the Supreme Court of Canada refused leave to appeal, so the Superior Court decision stood. To add insult to the financial injuries they had already sustained, the plaintiffs were ordered to pay legal fees that amounted to a whopping $440,000, or $20,000 each.

What all this boils down to is that if you decide to go into debt in order to get rich quick, you're on your own. The cavalry isn't going to charge in to save you if you run into trouble.

The Investment Funds Institute of Canada (IFIC) has warned that the practice of using leveraging to finance mutual fund purchases is on the rise, describing the misuse of the strategy as being contrary to the best interests of investors and potentially destabilizing for the mutual fund industry. In an advisory published in 2005, IFIC offered these tips to investors considering leveraging:

Ensure the investments bought with borrowed money are suitable in helping you meet your goals and objectives and fall within your risk tolerance levels.

Keep a sufficient financial cushion to see you through any declines. Ensure your cash flow permits you to continue loan payments.

Understand the risk of using collateral (i.e.: family home) as security for the loan. If the lender calls their loan and the value of your investments fall, you could lose that collateral.

Understand the tax consequences. The interest paid on borrowed money for investing can be a tax deduction but any realized profit may be taxed.

Borrow only an amount you can comfortably pay back even if the investment drops in value.

The Ontario Securities Commission has also tried to educate people about the dangers involved in leveraging by publishing a booklet titled "Borrowing to Invest," which is available online.[2] It contains a warning that the downside of using a line of credit to invest is "that you could be putting your equity, and possibly your home, at risk." It then goes on to offer a fictional example of a retired couple (the Smiths) who decide to take out a $100,000 mortgage on their paid-up home with the goal of earning enough to cover the mortgage payments and provide some extra income. They choose a mutual fund with a five-year average annual compound rate of return of more than 10 percent. However, past returns are no guarantee of future results. The stock market tanks and their fund loses 15 percent in the first year, leaving them with only $85,000 of the original $100,000, plus the interest cost on the mortgage. The booklet explains:

> The Smiths are now faced with a tough choice: sell some of their investment at a loss to make the mortgage payments, or sell their house and hope that what they get will be enough to pay off the mortgage, pay the real estate commissions and provide for somewhere else to live. Either way, they run the risk of losing money—and their home.

In case readers still miss the point, the booklet is illustrated with colourful graphics that include rolling dice and a house of cards.

At this point, you'd probably run screaming from the room the moment a financial advisor even whispered the words "loan" and "invest" in the same sentence. Most times you'd be right to do so. But there are a few occasions where leveraging makes sense, providing you go about it in the right way.

One example is an RRSP loan. They are widely available in January and February and are often offered at prime rate. These loans provide a way to top up your current year RRSP contribution if you're short of cash and/or to take advantage of carry-forward credits available to you. Unlike other types of investment loans, the interest costs are not tax deductible, however.

An RRSP loan is one of the few ways you can be absolutely certain you'll make money by leveraging—if you go about it correctly. That's because of the tax refund the loan will produce for you. Suppose you have $10,000 worth of RRSP contribution room and your marginal tax rate is 40 percent. You don't have the cash available so you borrow the money and invest it in a GIC that pays 5 percent interest. Your one-year return on the borrowed money will be a tax refund of $4,000 plus $500 in GIC interest for a total of $4,500. That's a 45 percent gain. Of course, you have to subtract the cost of the interest on the loan from that, but if you pay off the full balance over twelve months in equal instalments, the total interest charge will amount to $355.64, assuming a 6.5 percent interest rate. Leveraging has paid off big time.

There are only three rules you need to apply if you decide to do this:

1. Make sure you can comfortably handle the monthly loan payments.
2. Plan to pay off the entire loan within one year, two at the most. Beyond that, your returns will diminish because the interest rate on the loan is more than you are earning on the GIC.
3. Minimize the interest rate. There is a lot of competition in the RRSP loan market. Don't pay any more than you have to. You may even find a lender that is prepared to charge less than prime if you open your RRSP with that institution.

The higher your tax bracket, the better RRSP leveraging works because your refund will be more. If claiming the full contribution would drop you into a lower bracket, you can carry over a portion of the deduction to the following year (or further if you wish) in order to maximize the tax advantage.

The second leveraging strategy that may make sense for some people is to use money from a reverse mortgage for the financing. The advantage of this approach is that you don't risk the loss of your home if things go awry.[3] That allows you to sleep a little easier.

Here's how it works. Reverse mortgages, which are available to people age 60 and older, allow you to borrow up to 40 percent of the value of the equity in your home (the younger you are, the less you can borrow). No monthly repayments are required. Interest on the loan accrues over the years and the full amount—principal plus accumulated interest—becomes payable when the property is sold or the last surviving spouse dies. The lender cannot seize your home, even if the total debt exceeds its market value.

Proceeds from a reverse mortgage loan (like any type of loan) are not taxable and can be used in any way you wish. The interest rate charged on these loans is higher than you would pay on a conventional mortgage or a home equity line of credit, but if the money is invested you reduce the real expense because of interest deductibility.

Let's assume that a couple in their 70s finds themselves in a cash squeeze. They need some extra income each month but they don't want to move out of their home. So they decide to look into a reverse mortgage and discover they qualify for a loan of $200,000.

They invest this money in low-risk securities—a portfolio of GICs, government bonds, preferred shares, and the like. The yield isn't very high, say 5 percent. But that's enough to produce

$10,000 a year in new income. Moreover, it's tax-free. That's because the interest deductibility will more than offset the investment income, leaving them with zero tax to pay. Since they don't have to make any monthly repayments on the reverse mortgage, they end up with an additional $833.33 a month to spend, which hopefully will be enough to solve their cash flow problem.

The obvious danger in this plan is that they decide to go for higher returns, thereby adding more risk to the investment portfolio. I caution against giving in to this temptation. Set your sights low, make safety of principal the number one priority, and you'll do just fine with this strategy.

Also, don't lose sight of the fact that the piper—in this case the reverse mortgage company—will eventually have to be paid and the final bill will be high because of the accrued interest. In the meantime, though, our couple has some extra money to spend.

So leveraging isn't always bad. It can be a valuable financial tool in the right circumstances. But if you look at it as simply a way to get rich quick, you could be asking for trouble.

SLEEP-EASY ADVICE: With a few exceptions, leveraging is a sure-fire prescription for insomnia. Don't get talked into it.

Chapter 10

Sleep-Easy Tax Savings

Any one may so arrange his affairs that his taxes shall be as low as possible; he is not bound to choose that pattern which will best pay the Treasury; there is not even a patriotic duty to increase one's taxes.

—Judge Learned Hand

Years ago, when our children were young, we took them on a vacation in France. One morning we drove our rented Peugeot to a nearby village in Brittany, where we bought some freshly baked bread at the local boulangerie. As we drove home, the smell of the bread, which was still hot from the oven, filled the car with a delicious aroma. The kids in the back seat were unusually quiet, but we didn't think much of it. When we got back to the farmhouse, my wife retrieved the bread bag and found herself staring in amazement at a forlorn heel. The rest had been devoured by the kids during the drive. The smell had driven them into a feeding frenzy!

The moral of the story is that it doesn't matter how much bread you have when you leave the bakery. What counts is how much remains when you get home.

The same is true of your money. Too many people focus on total return, when all that really matters is how much you have to spend once the taxman has eaten his share. As Judge Learned Hand, one of America's greatest jurists, stated in the quote that opens this chapter, there is nothing unpatriotic about arranging your financial life in a way that will keep your taxes at an absolute minimum.

However, there is a certain irony in Judge Hand's comment in that it formed part of a ruling against a taxpayer named Evelyn Gregory who in 1928 had used a complex corporate reorganization to reduce her personal income for tax purposes by $10,000.[1] The judge's landmark ruling against Mrs. Gregory was later upheld by the U.S. Supreme Court, which said in its own ruling that the entire manoeuvre, while legal on the face of it, was "a contrivance" and a "devious form of conveyance masquerading as a corporate reorganization."

So perhaps to Judge Hand's comment we should add, "As long you don't push the envelope too far." That's the real message you need to remember if you want to keep the tax people from haunting your dreams. Unfortunately, human nature being what it is, smart promoters are constantly coming up with new schemes for beating the Canada Revenue Agency (CRA). In most cases, the people who get sucked into these deals end up in a pile of trouble.

For example, I constantly receive inquiries from people wanting to know more about so-called charitable organizations that promise big tax receipts for small donations. In some cases, the appeal is made even more enticing by a suggestion that the donated money will be used to reduce famine or combat disease in developing countries—save tax dollars while saving the world!

Based on the anecdotal evidence of the emails I get, numerous organizations are actively soliciting donations from Canadians by appealing to this combination of philanthropy and greed. One example that came to my attention involves donating to an organization that purchases pharmaceutical drugs to be sent to distressed regions of Africa. Through a series of complex financial manoeuvres, the donor ends up with a charitable receipt that significantly exceeds the amount actually contributed.

There are many variations on this idea, involving everything from comic books to art. But the underlying premise is always the same: give a little, deduct a lot.

The Canada Revenue Agency (CRA) has issued several warnings about these charitable tax shelters, but they apparently continue to flourish and draw people in. All I can say is that if you're tempted, think twice. Thousands of taxpayers have been reassessed for deductions based on receipts from these "charities," and more cases are ongoing as I write.

Some taxpayers have gone to court to fight the CRA's reassessments, and in at least one case they won what appeared to be a victory. In 1999, the Tax Court of Canada ruled in favour of three investors who filed a claim on behalf of 1,850 people who had donated to an art charity run by CVI Art Management. The scheme involved using donated money to purchase limited-edition prints. These prints were then appraised at higher prices and donated to charitable organizations, which in turn issued receipts based on the appraised values. One of the plaintiffs spent $8,667 for prints that were later donated to a university. He received a tax receipt for $29,400.

When the Tax Court of Canada upheld the plaintiffs' right to claim the deduction, it appeared to throw open the doors to donate-low, claim-high charities, and they began springing up across the country. However, in 2005, the Federal Court of Appeal overturned the ruling, saying that the entire transaction lacked credibility (shades of the Gregory case so long ago). Subsequently, in April 2006, the Supreme Court of Canada refused the plaintiffs' request to appeal, without comment. So the ruling of the Federal Court of Appeal stands.[2]

Despite the Court of Appeal ruling, many of these charity tax shelters continue to claim that their receipts are valid and will be accepted by the CRA. The tax department has repeatedly warned people that this is not the case, stating on its website that amendments to the Income Tax Act limit donations made after 2003 to a maximum of the donor's out-of-pocket costs.

Nonetheless, variations of these schemes continue to pop up. In an article in the June 2007 issue of *Investment Executive*, a publication directed at financial advisors, writer David Baines tells of interviewing one Vancouver promoter who claimed to have distributed $700 million worth of pharmaceuticals through a chartable organization in the previous five years. Assuming tax receipts were issued for those amounts, that adds up to a potentially huge revenue loss for Ottawa and the Government of British Columbia. No wonder both the Department of Finance and the CRA have been focusing increased attention on this area of charitable giving.

The CRA website contains a page that warns potential donors about the risks involved in "leveraged cash donations" and "buy-low, donate-high arrangements":

> Promoters of such shelters must obtain a tax shelter number from the Canada Revenue Agency (CRA). The CRA uses the tax shelter number to identify the tax shelter and its investors, but offers no guarantee that taxpayers will receive the proposed tax benefits.
>
> The CRA reviews all tax shelters to ensure that the tax benefits being claimed meet the requirements of the *Income Tax Act*. The CRA has audited many of these gifting arrange-

ments. Generally, the CRA reduces the amount of the tax credit to no more than the taxpayers' cash donation, and in many cases it is reduced to even less than that. In some cases the credit is reduced to zero. The CRA may also charge interest and penalties.[3]

Pay special attention to the second paragraph. By donating to one of these charities, you are effectively inviting an audit, with all the discomfort and potential risk that entails. How great is the risk? A bulletin on the CRA website says that as of the date of posting, the CRA had audited over 14,000 taxpayers who made donations to these shelters and disallowed $916 million worth of claims. That adds up to a lot of grief and sleepless nights!

So my advice to all the folks who keep writing to ask about these things is very simple: Proceed at your own risk. If you want to take the chance of having your account red-flagged in perpetuity for the sake of getting a bigger tax refund, go ahead. Personally, I don't like the odds. I'm giving my donations to the Salvation Army and the United Way.

Another common ploy, which has also incurred the wrath of the CRA, is the Tax-Free RRSP Withdrawal scheme. Unscrupulous promoters, especially in eastern Ontario and Quebec, have been preying on seniors by telling them they have a foolproof method of getting money out of registered plans without incurring the high taxes that would normally be assessed. One form of this scam involves using money in a self-directed RRSP to buy shares in a private company at an inflated price. The promoter then loans the taxpayer money equal to the amount invested, less fees, with the RRSP as security.

In a Taxpayer Alert posted on its website in 2005, the CRA warned the transaction could end up being very expensive:

Taxpayers … risk losing retirement savings AND the tax benefits of those claims," the warning states. "If an RRSP is used as security for a loan, the value of the RRSP has to be added to the taxpayer's taxable income. Similarly, if an RRSP is used to purchase shares of a private corporation, and the shares are not a "qualified investment" under the rules, then the value of the shares will be added to the RRSP holder's taxable income.

The warning cites a 2004 ruling by the Tax Court of Canada in which a Quebec resident named Chantal Dubuc appealed a CRA reassessment of her 1998 tax return after she fell victim to a tax-free withdrawal scheme.[4] Ms. Dubuc had invested $20,000 from her self-directed plan in shares of a private company. She then received a loan of $16,620 from an associated company, for which she was charged a fee in excess of $3,000 (that's how the promoters make their money). She had no intention of repaying the tax-free loan but instead used her RRSP as security, apparently with the idea that the shares it held would eventually be returned to the company to satisfy the debt. She was hit with a CRA audit (nightmare number one) and subsequently slapped with a reassessment after the tax department added another $20,000 to her 1998 income (nightmare number two). She appealed the ruling, based on her belief that the promoter was legitimate and on a claim she had been told by a CRA representative that the transaction was legal. She lost, even though the judge stated that he believed that she had acted in good faith and had not deliberately defrauded the government. As for the unnamed CRA employee who had supposedly told her it was okay to go ahead, no one could identify the person—and even if they could, it would not have mattered. Incorrect advice from the CRA is not an acceptable legal defence.

There are many more tax scams out there. If you want the latest updates, check out the CRA website.

I haven't recounted all these cases to discourage you from taking action to reduce your taxes. In fact, there are many ways to trim your tax bill without venturing into grey areas (or, worse, deliberately breaking the law.) One of the most effective is to make regular RRSP contributions. This may seem like a motherhood statement, and readers of my previous books will know that I've said it many times before. But the fact is that most Canadians don't make use of this universally available tax shelter. Statistics consistently show less than half of Canadians take advantage of this simple way to cut their taxes each year. That's a lot of tax-sheltering potential that's going begging.

Apart from RRSP contributions, the tax return is full of potential money-saving opportunities. The federal *Income Tax Guide* even contains tips designed to help people reduce the amount they owe, though most Canadians don't read them. One of the best tax-saving techniques is to use a high-quality software program to prepare your return, such as Intuit's QuickTax. These programs will automatically alert you to savings you may have overlooked.

Entire books have been written on the subject of taxes, with those by Evelyn Jacks and Tim Cestnick among the best. So I'm not going to attempt to provide a complete strategy guide here. However, here are a few recent changes to the tax laws that you may have missed and which offer new tax-cutting opportunities.

Two types of capital gains. As a result of a Liberal initiative that was later picked up by the Conservatives, there are now two types of dividends to report. You need to know which is which if you're going to save yourself some money.

Dividends paid by large, publicly traded Canadian corporations qualify for an enhanced dividend tax credit. Payments from companies that pay the small business tax rate are not eligible. The distinction is very important. Qualifying dividends are taxed at a much lower rate, which means you keep a lot more cash in your pocket. It's worth noting that it is possible for one spouse to claim all the dividends paid to a couple under certain conditions (see line 120 in the *General Tax Guide*). This is where a software program can be especially helpful; you'll be able to experiment with the various options to see which works best.

Age amount increased. The maximum age amount that a person 65 or older can claim at line 301 of the return has been increased. However, there are two catches. First, this is not a deduction but a credit, which is worth less unless you are in the lowest tax bracket. Second, the age amount is income tested. If your net income exceeds a certain amount ($30,936 for the 2007 tax year), you'll lose part or all of the credit.

Public transit credit. The 2006 federal budget contained a provision allowing commuters to claim a tax credit for the cost of public transit passes. Only monthly or longer passes qualify. If it works to your advantage, one spouse may claim the total amount. You don't have to send in your receipts, but keep them in case the Canada Revenue Agency ever asks.

Higher pension credit. The pension credit has been increased to $2,000 (from $1,000), and the good news is there is no income test. Anyone can make this claim. Qualifying income includes regular payments (not lump sum withdrawals) from registered pension plans, deferred profit sharing plans, and RRSP-funded annuities. There is no age requirement for these payments. Periodic payments from RRIFs, LIFs, LRIFs, and so on can be used for the credit if you have reached age 65 (or younger if the payments resulted from the death of a spouse). Government payments from the Canada and Quebec Pension Plans and Old Age Security are not eligible.

New child tax credit. Effective with the 2007 tax year, parents can claim a federal tax credit of $310 for each child (the amount will be indexed in future years).

Pension splitting. This is a huge gain for older Canadians. Starting with the 2007 tax year, couples are allowed to split pension income between them. (In Canada, "couples" includes common-law and same-sex relationships.) The tax savings could be in the thousands of dollars, depending on the circumstances. Let's look at one example.

In June 2007, I received this question:

> *I will soon retire at age 60 with 35 years of federal government service and will receive a superannuation pension of $70,000 per year for my years with the government. My wife will be 58 years old and will not receive any pension income as she had never paid into a plan (Canada Pension Plan excepted). Given our ages, will I be allowed to split my pension with her ($35,000 each)? Please advise me if there is an age limit on splitting my pension.*

According to the Department of Finance website, the answer to this reader's question is yes, he can split the income with his wife. In most cases, you must be 65 to qualify for pension splitting, but there is one major exception: Income from a registered pension plan may be split at any time. This case clearly falls into that category.

So how much tax might this couple save? Based on 2006 tax rates (which did not change much in 2007), an Ontario resident with taxable income of $35,000 would owe tax of $5,580 for an average tax rate of 15.94 percent. So a couple paying tax at that rate would owe $11,160 between them. A person with taxable income of $70,000 would be assessed $16,556, for an average tax rate of 23.65 percent. Leaving all other income, deductions, and credits out of the calculation, the pension-splitting savings in this case is $5,396. That would pay for a very nice cruise holiday.

Since this book is titled *Sleep-Easy Investing,* I would be remiss not to include information on reducing taxes on investment income in this chapter. The first thing to keep in mind is that interest income takes the worst hit from the CRA. Interest is the only type of Canadian-generated investment income that does not get a tax break. You are taxed at your marginal rate (which could be in excess of 48 percent) on the full amount. There used to be a deduction for the first $1,000 of interest income received, but that is long gone.

Suppose your marginal tax rate is 40 percent and you hold an interest-bearing security paying 5 percent in a non-registered account. After taxes, your actual return is only 3 percent—the government took the other 2 percent for itself. With inflation running at 2.2 percent at the time of writing, your real return in spending power terms is reduced to 0.8 percent. Going back to my kids and the loaf of bread—you've been left with the heel.

The best way to protect yourself is to keep all your interest-bearing securities inside a registered plan (RRSP or RRIF) if at all possible. The money will be taxed when it eventually comes out, but in the meantime you'll be able to compound your interest income in a tax-sheltered environment.

So what should you hold in a taxable account? Dividend-paying securities should certainly be part of the mix. For example, a British Columbia resident with taxable income of $50,000 will pay a rate of only 4.4 percent on dividends from large Canadian companies. If that person's taxable income is only $35,000, the tax rate is zero. That's right, the dividends are tax-free![5]

Some people are wary of dividends because it means investing in the stock market. That's true, so there is risk involved. However, if you follow the guidelines I explained in Chapter 7 for minimizing stock market risk, you'll sleep better at night.

Real estate investment trusts (REITs) are another good source of tax-advantaged cash flow. These trusts use depreciation and amortization expenses to tax shelter a portion of their annual distributions, thus providing investors with enhanced after-tax returns. For example, in 2006, H&R REIT, one of the country's largest, reported total distributions of $1.33 per unit. Of that, almost half (48.3 percent) was not taxable in that year.

You can also find numerous mutual funds that have been structured so as to minimize taxes. Fidelity's T-SWP program is one example. Fidelity gives investors a choice on the amount of income they can receive. The S5 units provide for monthly withdrawals at an annualized rate of 5 percent from the fund of your choice, while the S8 units use an 8 percent target. Both are highly tax-efficient. To illustrate, in 2006 the S8 units of the Fidelity Canadian Balanced Fund paid out $1.69 each. Of that, 62 percent was tax-deferred return of capital, and 30 percent was tax-advantaged capital gains and dividends. Only 8 percent was fully taxable. The Fidelity Canada website provides a useful T-SWP calculator that enables you to quickly see how much income will be generated from the fund of your choice and the amount that will be classified as return of capital for tax purposes.[6]

Note that payments received as return of capital must be deducted from your original purchase price to create an adjusted cost base, or ACB. The ACB will be used to calculate your capital gains tax when you sell the units, so you or your estate will eventually have to repay a portion of the deferred tax. However, that may be many years in the future.

These are just a few examples of the many tax-saving possibilities out there. You don't have to wave a red flag in front of the CRA to ensure that you don't end up with the heel!

> **SLEEP-EASY ADVICE:** Steer clear of aggressive charities and other questionable schemes that purport to cut your tax bill. There are plenty of legal ways to save tax dollars. Why toss and turn at night worrying that tomorrow's mail may bring a notice of reassessment from Ottawa?

Chapter 11

The Retirement Follies

Retirement at sixty-five is ridiculous. When I was sixty-five, I still had pimples.

—George Burns

All the surveys tell the same story. Most Canadians want to retire early, preferably before age 60. They believe that's a reasonable goal and that they'll have enough money to achieve it. It's not that they're unhappy with their jobs, most of them tell pollsters. It's just that they want to enjoy what they often describe as "the good life."

Welcome to the Retirement Follies, featuring a starry-eyed generation of baby boomers who for the most part don't have a clue what's coming. Unless these self-contented folks wake up in a hurry, they are going to experience many sleepless nights in the future.

Don't take my word for it. Listen to the Canadian Institute of Actuaries. These people are the number-crunchers who spend their lives figuring out what the chances are that you'll be involved in a car accident or die within the next 10 years. In June 2007, they published a report titled *Planning for Retirement: Are Canadians*

Saving Enough? The findings may come as a shock to people who think they are adequately prepared for the financial challenges of aging. "Two thirds of Canadian households expecting to retire in 2030 are not saving at levels required to meet necessary living expenses," the report concludes.

> Old Age Security (OAS) and the Canada and Quebec Pension Plans (C/QPP) provide a modest base, and by them-selves, are not designed to fill the gap. Home ownership will help to narrow the gap, but, by itself, won't be enough. Participation in a workplace pension plan (RPP), by itself, won't be enough. And, saving through a Registered Retirement (Savings) Plan (RRSP) plays an important role, but is unlikely to fill the gap.[1]

What will it take to fill these gaps? Personal savings, to the extent that most people probably won't be able to afford it. The actuaries say that a couple, both age 40, earning $40,000 a year who hopes to retire in 25 years, at age 65, needs to put aside 30 percent of their gross income every year in order to have enough just to cover non-discretionary expenses (in other words, the basic costs of sustaining life) when they retire, assuming a low level of inflation. That's $12,000 annually! How many people at that income level can afford to save that much? Darn few. And the actu-aries stress that if people want some extra money to be able to afford some fun (the aforementioned "good life") after they stop work, they need to save even more.

The only alternative, say the actuaries, is to put off retirement, perhaps for several years. If our couple delays retirement until age 68, the amount of their income that they need to save annually falls to 21 percent. If they wait until age 73, they only need to save

6 percent a year, or $2,400. Now we're getting into the realm of reality.

Not surprisingly, the actuaries found that the higher your income, the lower the percentage you have to put aside. A couple earning $80,000 annually needs to save only 12 percent of gross income to retire in 25 years. Still, that amounts to $9,600 a year, which would probably be a stretch for most people in that income category. If they postpone retirement to age 73, the annual savings requirement falls to 5 percent.

Taking everything into account, the report concludes that two-thirds of Canadian households are not saving at the rate needed to meet basic expense needs at retirement. That's a very worrisome statistic.

Here's another one. When Fidelity Investments Canada published its 2006–07 Canadian Retirement Survey, Peter Drake, the company's vice-president of economic and retirement research, suggested that the new retirement savings target should be between 75 and 85 percent of pre-retirement income (the traditional benchmark established by the federal government several years ago was 70 percent). The reason: "People in retirement have higher aspirations. They want to travel, be involved in new activities, and may well change the place they live." Ergo, they'll need more money.

It may be that while many Canadians are still wearing rose-coloured glasses when it comes to retirement planning, there is an increasing, but perhaps still subliminal, awareness that things are not likely to work out exactly as expected. The Fidelity study found that an astonishing 77 percent of respondents who are still in the labour force plan to continue working after they "retire." While the majority said they would work full- or part-time for an employer, almost one-third said they would go into consulting or start their own business.

Those numbers are wildly out of sync with current reality. A survey conducted on behalf of Desjardins Financial Security and published in October 2006 found that only 8 percent of Canadians who were retired at the time actually continue to work.

This suggests that the Fidelity results are more a prediction of the future than a reflection of the past. Increasingly, we're hearing about the strains that will be placed on public services as baby boomers retire, a phenomenon that has already started. (In Canada, the baby boom generation began in 1947.) We were warned by then–Bank of Canada governor David Dodge in June 2007 that as the population ages, employment in Canada will decrease, which will in turn slow national economic growth.

In the United States, no less a personage than Alan Greenspan, the highly respected former chairman of the Federal Reserve Board, told conference attendees in New York in April 2007 that we are about to experience a demographic shift that is "unique in world history." In a report published on the Advisor.ca website, he was quoted as saying: "The notion of people retiring and people living some semblance of life is a relatively new phenomenon. We've ... succeeded in handling (retirement) up to this point. But now ... a large chunk of the work force is going to move from a state of contributing to becoming recipients. I don't think we are ready for this."

This is serious stuff.

Many provincial governments have already taken steps to encourage aging baby boomers to stay on the job by repealing mandatory retirement laws. (Interestingly, Greenspan was about two months shy of his 80th birthday when he stepped down as head of the Fed.) But sheer financial necessity may be the ultimate driving force as people start to realize that they don't have the financial resources to quit work and live that good life they've always dreamed about.

One reason the dream is out of reach for many is the demise of private-sector pension plans. Most public-service employees participate in generous defined benefit pension plans, which ensure them a level of retirement income commensurate with their length of service and salary. But these plans are going the way of the dinosaur in the private sector because of high costs and bureaucratic red tape.

The actuaries' report concluded that a single person who contributed to a defined benefit plan for 25 years or more would receive a pension which, when combined with CPP/QPP and OAS payments, would provide enough money to meet basic household costs. No additional savings would be needed. That's the power of a defined benefit (DB) plan. If you have one, sleep easy!

Unfortunately, based on 2004 statistics, only one-third of Canadians in the $30,000 to $40,000 income range have a DB plan. The figure rose to 43 percent for people earning $80,000 or more, but that's still less than half the population in that income category. Says the actuaries' report: "The rate of participation in DB plans in the public sector is approximately 80 percent, while the rate in the private sector is marginally over 20 percent. Statistic Canada's Pension Plans in Canada survey indicated that 39 percent of paid workers were covered by a registered pension plan in 2004—down from 45.3 percent in 1991."[2]

So it appears that the secret to a comfortable retirement is to get a job in the public sector. Failing that, here are some suggestions of ways in which you can beat the odds and achieve the dream.[3]

Start early. If you're under 40 when you read this (or, even better, under 30), you can reduce the retirement savings burden dramatically by starting to put aside money immediately. The longer you delay, the tougher it gets.

The numbers are truly mind-boggling. TD Canada Trust offers a valuable online retirement calculator that allows you to plug in your figures to see how much of a difference an early start can make.[4] I used a scenario that assumed a target retirement income of $40,000 a year, an average annual inflation rate of 2 percent, an average annual compound rate of return of 8 percent, retirement at age 65, and no pension plan. The income would have to last for 25 years. Here's what the computer spit out: A 45-year-old would need to save slightly more than $13,000 yearly in an RRSP to build the financial base needed (assuming no RRSP savings to that point). By increasing the target retirement age to 70 and reducing the number of years for which the income would be required to 20, the required annual RRSP contribution dropped about 40 percent, to just over $8,000.

Using the same assumptions, a 35-year-old would need to save $6,120 a year to retire at age 65 with a $40,000 income. A 25-year-old would need to put aside only $3,154.

If you're already too old to benefit from this information, make sure your children read this section!

Be realistic. Almost everyone seems to want to retire before age 60. But how realistic is that? Unless you have already put aside a large amount of money (I'm talking $100,000 or more), early retirement is a virtual impossibility for anyone who does not have a DB pension plan or a large inheritance coming. Maybe that's why so many people buy lottery tickets.

Let's go back to the 45-year-old from the previous example. We'll now assume he's already saved $50,000 in an RRSP and wants to retire at age 60 with enough capital to generate $40,000 annually for 25 years. The TD Canada Trust calculator tells us he'd need to save a whopping $15,720 a year to achieve that goal. Even if his

RRSP was currently worth $100,000, he'd still have to contribute almost $11,000 to the plan every year.

If savings on that level (or whatever level you need to achieve your personal goal) are out of your reach, it's best to find out now. Don't wait until your planned retirement date is five years away to discover that the dream and the reality don't mesh. Once you have the stark numbers in front of you, make whatever adjustments are needed to bring the plan into line with what you can afford. It may mean reducing your hoped-for standard of living, or postponing your planned retirement date, or sacrificing some luxuries now to save more for later. None of those are easy decisions, but any of them is preferable to the shock of waking up one morning after you retire and discovering you're broke.

Don't take undue risks. Increasing the average annual return on your RRSP savings can significantly reduce the amount of money you need to put aside each year. For example, our 35-year-old needed to save $6,120 a year to reach his retirement objective if his annual return was 8 percent. But if he could increase that return to 10 percent, the required yearly saving drops all the way to $3,557. At a 12 percent return, it's down to $2,079. Obviously, there's a powerful incentive to shoot for better returns and keep some of that RRSP money for other purposes.

There's just one problem—risk. The higher the target rate of return from any investment, the greater the implied risk. For each percentage point of return potential you add, the odds that you will suffer a material loss at some stage shorten. Never lose sight of the fact that an RRSP is really a pension plan. As such, a primary goal should be to never lose money. There's a reason why professional pension plan managers invest conservatively. They would rather see a gradual increase in the plan's value each year than risk a big loss from which it could take a long time to recover.

Here's an example. Suppose you invested $10,000 in an RRSP, putting the money in equity mutual funds. Over the subsequent four years, you lost 10 percent in the first year, gained 11 percent in the second, lost 9 percent in the third, and gained 10 percent in the fourth. So the percentage gains have always been greater than the losses. Are you ahead or behind at that point?

Actually, you've just about broken even. After four years on the see-saw, your plan is worth a penny less than it was when you started. At that kind of growth rate, you can forget about ever retiring.

If, instead of the mutual funds, you had chosen a boring GIC paying 5 percent, your plan would have been worth $12,155 after four years for a total advance of more than 21 percent. As a bonus, you would have slept better. This is not an argument for putting everything into GICs. Rather, the point is not to overreach for return, however tempting it may be to do so.

Be disciplined. For many people, retirement saving is hit or miss. If there's some cash available at RRSP time, then okay, I'll dump it into the plan. If not, too bad—I'll make it up next year.

You'll never meet your retirement goals that way. The most effective method of retirement savings if you don't have a pension plan is to set up an automatic contribution plan with an advisor or a financial institution. Give instructions to your bank to contribute a percentage of every paycheque to the RRSP and provide clear directions as to how the money is to be invested. After a pay raise or two, you won't even notice the money is coming off the top, but your RRSP will be steadily growing.

SLEEP-EASY ADVICE: When it comes to retirement realities, many Canadians fall into the blissfully ignorant category. They have no idea what it will take in financial terms to achieve what in many cases is an unreasonable goal. The first-stage cure for ignorance of any type is education. Find out the facts, however jarring they may be. Then you can begin the process of putting a workable plan into place.

Chapter 12

Panic Attacks

Each is liable to panic, which is exactly, the terror of ignorance surrendered to the imagination.
—Ralph Waldo Emerson

The great American poet and philosopher Ralph Waldo Emerson was not thinking about the stock market in 1870 when he penned the line that opens this chapter as part of his essay titled "Courage." But his words fit like a glove. The great financial panics of history in the end boil down to the "terror of ignorance surrendered to the imagination."

Emerson's choice of words was brilliant because they speak directly to human psychology and to one of the great perils of investing. When confronted with distressing news that we do not understand, we allow our imaginations to conjure up the worst possible outcome. The fear generated by that process then prompts us to take action that under more rational circumstances we would never contemplate.

I have seen it happen many times in many forms over the years. It's not just stocks that are subject to collective panic attacks on the part of investors; it has happened to bonds, income trusts, currencies, real estate, gold—in fact, just about every form of wealth that exists. Whenever people feel their personal assets are at risk, the immediate reaction of most is to panic and sell. Usually, that panic is born of ignorance—they just don't understand what's going on.

One small example of that occurred on February 27, 2007. On that day, the Shanghai stock market suffered a major meltdown, losing 8.8 percent of its valuation and wiping out about $100 billion in capitalization. Stocks around the world immediately plunged as panicky investors scrambled to sell, fearing the Shanghai surprise signalled the start of a new bear market. The closely watched Dow Jones Industrial Average dropped 416 points (3.3 percent), forcing the White House to issue a statement saying the U.S. government was closely monitoring the situation. That probably had the effect of unnerving investors even more. It was a similar story in Europe, where stocks were battered unmercifully. U.S. investors were showing "a degree of panic," said market strategist David Fuller.

What exactly were they panicking about? In most cases, they hadn't a clue. They'd heard on the news that a Chinese stock market had gone into free fall. That immediately conjured up memories of the 1997 Asian financial crisis that spread around the world and produced the biggest one-day drop in the history of the New York Stock Exchange, on October 27. (The speed at which the crisis spread earned it the nickname "Asian flu.")

In fact, there was no similarity between the two events. The 2007 correction really was a case of ignorance surrendering to imagination. The 1997 sell-off at least had some tangible underlying causes.

The 1997 financial Asian flu was the culmination of a series of events, spread over several months. It actually started in July of that year in South Korea with the bankruptcy of Kia Motors and in Thailand with the collapse of its currency, the baht. It became apparent to the U.S. government (although not to the general public) that Thailand's central bank was in deep trouble because of sky-high interest rates, a pegged exchange rate, and rapidly depleting reserves, and efforts were made behind the scenes to contain the damage. But when the malaise spread to South Korea's central bank, anxieties grew because of the large loan exposure of Japanese and European financial institutions to that country. The domino effect took hold, with other Asian nations, such as Indonesia, Malaysia, Singapore, and the Philippines, showing the effect of the financial squeeze. Finally, the lid blew off the pressure cooker in October, and markets around the world tumbled. It took the better part of a year for investors to regain confidence, and it would probably have taken much longer had it not been for the onset of the high-tech craze.

The events of February 2007 were totally different. The Shanghai stock market is a domestic exchange which by and large is open only to Chinese nationals. It is tightly controlled by the government, which means that the slightest policy twitch can have a huge impact on prices. Because it is not a free market, its gyrations should have no effect on investors in Toronto, New York, or London. However, many people didn't realize that. They had read in the papers and seen on the news many stories about the tremendous growth in China and how important the country was becoming on the world economic scene. To wake up one morning and hear on the radio that the largest stock market in the country (excluding Hong Kong, which is a free market) had lost almost 9 percent overnight was enough to send thousands of people to their phones or computers with sell orders. Ignorance surrendering to imagination.

Once the business media explained the realities of the Shanghai market, investor confidence quickly returned. By mid-April the Dow was back to its pre-crash level and went on from there to new all-time highs. And what about the people who had dumped their shares in February? They had learned an expensive lesson: Never sell into a panic. Realizing after the fact that you made a stupid move is a sure way to guarantee a lot of sleepless nights.

As a footnote to the February correction, in late June 2007 the Shanghai market fell 21 percent in the space of four days. The rest of the world yawned and went about its business. The headline in the *Toronto Star* of July 3 summed it up neatly: "Retreat of Chinese stocks barely noticed in the West." Investors were no longer over-reacting out of ignorance.

A similar phenomenon occurred in the bond markets back in 1987 (for some reason, it seems that years ending in seven are rough ones for investors). On October 19 of that year (what is it about October, anyway?), the Dow fell more than 500 points, wiping out $500 billion in personal wealth in a single day. Almost unnoticed in the Wall Street carnage was a corresponding plunge in the bond markets, triggered by a panic-driven sell-off of high-yield, low-quality junk bonds. The selling frenzy quickly spread to government bonds. Except for short-term speculators, this didn't make much sense, because government bonds are guaranteed for principal and interest, and the risk of default is almost non-existent in the case of bonds issued by stable countries such as Canada and the United States. But many investors didn't understand the distinction. They heard that bond prices were falling and wanted to get out.

That was the time when a woman called into a Vancouver phone-in show on which I was a guest and asked if she should sell her bond fund. It happened to be with Phillips, Hager & North, which has one of the best bond management teams in the country.

I did everything possible to talk her out of the idea, assuring her that she would not lose her savings by keeping her fund units and that the bond market correction was a passing event. She still seemed dubious when she hung up. Of course, the bond market did recover, and her bond fund performed very well in the subsequent years. Over the two decades to May 31, 2007, the Phillips, Hager & North Bond Fund posted an average annual compound rate of return of 8.74 percent. Had she sold in 1987, she would have taken a loss on her investment and missed out on all the prosperous years that followed.

The bear market of 2000–02 produced not one but two panic attacks. The first occurred in late 2000 when investors suddenly woke up to the fact that the high-tech bubble had really burst and sold off their dot-com stocks for anything they could get. The NASDAQ Composite Index crashed from a level of more than 4,000 in late summer to about 2,500 by year's end. It continued to fall from there until fall 2002, though at a more gradual pace.

The broader U.S. indexes and the TSX managed to hold up reasonably well in the face of the NASDAQ carnage, and for a while it was thought that the damage could be confined to the high-tech sector. But in summer 2002, after several corrections and recoveries, investor confidence snapped. The Dow, which had been over 10,000 in May, fell all the way to the 7,200 range in October in what turned out to be the bear market's culminating sell-off. It was a similar story in Toronto, where the S&P/TSX Composite Index slid from almost 8,000 in March to below 5,700 in October, a frightening decline of 29 percent in about six months.

As always happens, it was the people who lost their nerve and sold near the bottom who were hurt the worst. The markets rallied back strongly in 2003, with the TSX gaining more than 24 percent that year.

We don't have to go any farther back in time than November 2006 for an example of a made-in-Canada panic attack. As mentioned in Chapter 7, on Halloween night of that year, Finance Minister Jim Flaherty shocked the investment world by announcing that his Conservative government would slap a tax of 31.5 percent on distributions from income trusts, effective January 1, 2011. His rationale was that the burgeoning income trust sector had become a drain on federal tax revenues and the pending conversion of Telus, BCE, and EnCana to trust status would transform a worrisome situation into a crisis. Despite a specific campaign promise not to tax income trusts, he said his government had no choice but to act.

Predictably, the knee-jerk response was to panic. The situation was exacerbated by the fact that most income trust units were held by small investors, many of them retirees, who were lacking in stock market savvy. They had bought the trusts for yield at a time of low interest rates, and now the government was unexpectedly changing all the rules. Many of them wasted no time in stampeding for the exits. By two o'clock on the afternoon of November 1, the S&P/TSX Composite Index, which had integrated income trusts into the system only a few months previous, was down more than three hundred points.

Having seen similar phenomena before, I immediately sent out a bulletin to the subscribers to all my email newsletters, urging them to stay calm. I wrote:

Picking up your phone now and telling your broker to bail out isn't the solution. You just risk making a bad situation worse. In situations such as this, the markets are immediately swamped with sell orders and there are few buyers. That kind of supply-demand imbalance drives prices down to unrealistic lows. Would-be sellers who enter market orders (orders to sell at whatever price a buyer will pay) in such situations risk being taken out at prices well below what their shares will be worth when conditions stabilize....

My advice is to sit tight.... Give the markets time to regain stability and a sense of proportion. You won't avoid losing money by being patient, but you'll be able to mitigate your losses and do some intelligent tax planning.... For now, my best advice is to keep your cool.

As it turned out, I was overly pessimistic in my comments when I said that investors would not be able to avoid losing at least some of their money. Initially, they took a big collective hit, with the income trust sector losing an estimated $30 billion in market capitalization in the days immediately following the announcement. But then trusts began to rally as the bargain hunters (some might call them vultures) swooped in. Although the S&P/TSX Capped Income Trust Index never did get back to its pre-Flaherty highs, it did gain 5.4 percent in the first half of 2007. The trust tax also spawned a rash of takeover deals from which investors profited handsomely.

One example is the April 2007 takeover of Gateway Casinos Income Fund, which operates seven casinos in British Columbia and Alberta, by Australia's New World Gaming Partners, a joint venture owned by Publishing and Broadcasting Ltd. and Macquarie Bank. Investors saw the value of their holdings soar by almost 26 percent after the trust announced it had accepted a takeover offer of $25.26 per unit, placing a total value of about $800 million on the fund. The people who resisted the temptation to panic and hung on to their Gateway shares after the trust market plunged in early November were richly rewarded for sticking it out.

The share price had fallen as low as $14.50 after the Flaherty announcement. The takeover bid was 74 percent higher than that and represented a 25.7 percent premium over the closing price of $20.03 on the day before the news was released. In fact, the Australian offer topped the highest trading price in the history of the trust.

Gateway was not an isolated case. Many other income trusts were snapped up at premium prices, often by foreign buyers, during the spring and early summer of 2007. They included KCP Income Fund, Great Lakes Carbon Income Fund, Lakeport Brewing Income Fund, Entertainment One Income Fund, Amtelecom Income Fund, UE Waterheater Income Fund, VOXCOM Income Fund, Clean Power Income Fund, E.D. Smith Income Fund, and several others. Investors who had dumped their shares the previous November at distressed prices were left crying on the sidelines while those that had stuck it out reaped some unexpected but very welcome profits.

Panic attacks aren't confined to broad markets. Individual securities are vulnerable to them at any time. All it takes is some bad news. The shares of Merck & Company were cruising along comfortably in the US$45 range in late September 2004 when the U.S. pharmaceutical giant suddenly announced that it was pulling its multi-billion-dollar arthritis drug VIOXX off the market because studies showed it increased the risk of strokes and heart attacks among some patients. The stock price plunged by more than US$12 the next day on a huge volume of 145 million shares—a clear indication that institutional investors had been swept up in the panic.

As almost always happens in such situations, this was exactly the time to buy. As John D. Rockefeller Sr. once famously put it: "The way to make money is to buy when blood is running in the streets." Merck shares gradually rallied back to their pre-VIOXX level and by spring 2007 were trading in the US$55 range.

It's easy enough for me to tell you not to panic when the going gets tough. But it is very difficult to sit still when the newspaper headlines and the television newscasts are screaming that a major financial crisis is underway. Hype tends to trump reason in such circumstances. The best way to avoid panic is to not create a situation in which it is likely to happen. Panic-proof your investments. There are three ways to achieve this. The first is to avoid bubble investing—it always ends badly. The second is to take some profits when stock market indexes hit new records. Often a correction is close behind. The third is to carefully assess the amount of risk you are willing to accept and structure your investment portfolio accordingly. In Chapter 16, I'll explain how to do this.

SLEEP-EASY ADVICE: Panic selling is a surefire way to lose money. It won't be easy at the time, but toughing it out will pay off in the long run.

Chapter 13

The Pursuit of Safety

Everyone knows that if you are too careful you are so occupied in being careful that you are sure to stumble over something.
—Gertrude Stein

The bear market that began this century did more than wipe out a big chunk of many people's retirement savings. It appears to have psychologically scarred a generation, if not for life, then at least for decades.

How else can we explain the frantic pursuit of safety that we've seen in the years since the tech bust? A large number of people have become so consumed with avoiding loss that they have spawned an entirely new breed of security: the principal-protected note. In the process, they have generated millions of dollars in fees and commissions for brokers and underwriters who continue to roll out new issues of these questionable products on a weekly basis.

Now, there is nothing wrong with being prudent when it comes to investing. No less an expert on the subject than multi-billionaire Warren Buffett neatly summed it up when he defined the two most important rules for financial success: "Rule number one: Never lose money. Rule number two: Never forget rule number one."

That's sound advice, but I suspect the Oracle of Omaha, as Buffett has come to be known, would agree that it can be taken too far. He would probably concur with the great World War II general, Douglas MacArthur, who was quoted as saying: "There is no security on this earth; there is only opportunity." As in all things, moderation is the key to financial success. Anyone who becomes fixated on a single goal risks paying dearly for it in other ways. That's exactly what has happened since 2002 as safety has muscled out every other consideration in the minds of many people.

Financial companies have become remarkably innovative. They spin out new products almost before people realize they want them, usually with remarkable success. In this case, they were quick to seize on the trauma created by the bear market and provide investors with a product that no one had ever heard of before and which few people to this day really understand.

It wasn't always this way. A generation ago, the financial services industry in Canada consisted of little more than the good, grey banks and several third-rate stock markets. Most people kept any extra money they had in cookie jars or savings accounts. For those who were adventurous enough to "invest," the most popular securities were guaranteed investment certificates (GICs) and Canada Savings Bonds, the latter being the gift of choice for kids who already had closets full of toys.

The stock market was a kind of sophisticated gambling casino for high rollers. Mutual funds were barely a blip on the horizon. Hedge funds, limited partnerships, exchange-traded funds (ETFs), stripped bonds, and income trusts had yet to be invented.

Simpler times, indeed. Of course, no one worried too much about saving in those days. Just earning enough to meet the day-to-day living expenses was challenge enough. Retirement planning was almost unheard of. If you lived long enough to earn a gold watch, the company pension plan would take care of you. Failing that, the kids could pitch in—after all, you supported them for years, didn't you?

My, how the world has changed. Today, we're faced with a dazzling array of investment options. Simplicity has given way to opacity as people struggle to understand the myriad choices available in the financial marketplace and try to decide which ones are best suited to their needs. Blame the Bay Street innovators and their complicit marketers for this state of affairs. They have become experts at inventing clever new products and then hyping the hell out of them.

In recent years, these market manipulators realized that the pursuit of safety had become the main financial objective for older people. Since the population is aging, with the leading edge of the baby boom generation now coming up to retirement, older folks now count for a lot when it comes to selling financial products and services. That this generation controls most of the country's personal wealth only adds to the allure. What these people want above all else is security. They are the classic candidates for a risk-free approach to investing, and the Bay Street innovators have been working overtime to give them exactly what they want.

Of course, older people have always tended to be conservative by nature when it comes to money. But that natural inclination was magnified by the millennium bear market of 2000–02. The high-tech meltdown was all the more shocking because of the rampant euphoria that immediately preceded it. The collapse of the Soviet Union, the end of the Cold War, the advent of the internet, a new era of low interest rates, and booming real estate prices all combined to create a climate of boundless optimism about the future. Everything old was really old! We were experiencing a "paradigm shift" that was taking humankind onto a new plane of prosperity. (Funny, we don't hear much about paradigm shifts any more, even though we are actually living through several of them simultaneously, including the rise of China and India and the growing spectre of global warming.)

When the millennium bear market hit, it caught most people completely by surprise. What started as a meltdown in the high-tech sector eventually infected the stock markets around the world. As we have seen in earlier chapters, malaise escalated to distress, which eventually culminated in panic in the early fall of 2002 as investors dumped stocks and equity funds in a classic sell-off that drove markets to lows not seen since the 1970s. In the process, savings were decimated and retirement plans shattered. In the midst of this destruction of wealth came the attack on the World Trade Center. The unbounded optimism of the 1990s degenerated into a climate of pessimism and fear, from which has evolved an all-consuming pursuit of safety. Bay Street saw it all and decided that it was good—good for their business, that is.

The bear market ended in October 2002, and by mid-2007 every major world index except NASDAQ and the Tokyo Nikkei was hitting new record highs, and even NASDAQ was finally showing signs of recovery. But many people didn't care. They had become so demoralized by the losses of 2000–02 that all they were concerned about was preserving what they had left. Of course, that didn't mean greed had disappeared from the financial equation. It never does. But now people were demanding that a safety component be added to their desire for more wealth. In effect, they were asking for greed without risk.

It's an improbable combination but nothing seems to be beyond the wit of our financial geniuses. They responded with principal-protected notes (PPNs), a hybrid product that offers a chance at big gains while ensuring that, if things go wrong, you won't lose your stake. It's something like sitting down at a roulette table with a guarantee that, at worst, your stack of chips won't be any smaller when it's time to go to bed.

The public embraced the idea. By mid-2007, Canadians had collectively poured an estimated $14 billion into more than 600 PPN issues.

They clearly loved the idea of being able to place a bet on the future direction of the stock market, or on a bundle of mutual funds, or on commodity indexes without really seeming to risk anything. Greed with safety! How can you go wrong?

Easily, in fact. PPNs are a terrific invention for brokers and underwriters, many of whom pad their bank accounts with fat sales commissions and fees. For everyone else, they're a crap shoot. And yes, you can lose on these things if you take inflation and the time value of money into account.

PPNs are actually a direct descendant of a product that first appeared in the late 20th century, the market-linked GIC. As interest rates declined through the mid-1980s and into the 1990s, people began to cash in low-yielding GICs and move their money into mutual funds. GICs had been a huge business for the banks, and they knew something had to be done to stop the bleeding. The response was the market-linked GIC, which based its return not on interest rates but on the movement of an under-lying stock index, such as what was then known as the TSE 300, over the term of the note. Like regular GICs, the investor's principal was guaranteed at maturity. But unlike traditional GICs, there was no guarantee of return. If the benchmark index did well over the term, you made money. If it dropped, you got your principal back but nothing more. So it was possible that you could tie up your capital for as long as five years with zero profit at the end.

That's exactly what happened to people who bought these securities in the late 1990s or in early 2000. Using a handy calculator on the Royal Bank's website,[1] I found that a five-year investment made on March 31, 2000, in either its Canadian or Global market-linked GICs would have returned zero at maturity. Think about that—five years and nothing to show for it. Sure, you would have received your money back, but the purchasing power would have been reduced by five years of inflation. That's no way to build wealth.

Of course, if your timing had been better, the story would be different. A three-year investment in Royal's Canadian market-linked GIC made on March 31, 2003, just as the new bull market was gaining traction, would have produced a profit of 18.33 percent at maturity in 2006. But that's total return. On an average annual compounded basis, your money would have earned only about 5.8 percent a year. By comparison, one of Royal's more conservative mutual funds, RBC Balanced Fund, posted annual gains of 14.4 percent, 8.1 percent, and 14.7 percent during the same period. Yes, there was a risk of loss, but it was small compared with the returns.

Still, that small risk was enough to convince a lot of people that the market-linked GIC was preferable. Now many of those same people have moved on to the much more complex world of PPNs in the hope of better profits—still with zero risk, of course.

Like market-linked GICs, a simple PPN will track the performance of a recognized stock index, such as the S&P/TSX Composite or the Standard & Poor's 500, which is made up of the largest five hundred companies in the United States. And again, as with market-linked GICs, you tie up your money for three or five years,

at the end of which time you receive a return based on the performance of the index over that period. Nothing all that different so far.

However, unlike market-linked GICs, PPNs come with a lot of
extra costs attached. In fact, the only sure winners are the underwriters of the issue and the broker or dealer who sells it to you.
They get their fees and commissions right off the top—typically 3
to 5 percent of the total amount raised, but sometimes more. If the
commission is 5 percent, only $95 out of every $100 you invest
actually goes to work for you. Of that amount, a significant
percentage, perhaps as much as 70 percent of the total, goes to
purchasing a strip bond or a forward contract that provides the
"guarantee" that your capital will be returned to you at maturity.
The organization that provides the guarantee is known as the
"counterparty"—a term you need to understand if you invest in
PPNs.

Your upfront cost is probably not your only expense. Most
PPNs also have annual fees and expenses attached. I have seen
management expense ratios (MERs) as high as 2.65 percent, and
some may be even higher than that. Some of that money is paid as
a trailer fee to financial advisors, thus providing another incentive
to sell the product. But costs aren't the only problem. Here are
some of my other concerns about PPNs.

Long lock-in. I've seen some notes with maturity dates more than
eight years away. That's far too long to lose access to your money.
A lot can happen during eight years, or even three.

Poor transparency. You can track the performance of any stock
you own on a minute-to-minute basis. Most mutual fund NAVs
(net asset values) are updated daily. But try to figure out exactly
where your PPN investment stands at any given time. In some

cases, the results aren't published anywhere, and you probably won't be able to work it out yourself, even with a calculator. However, you can find some PPN results at Globefund.com in the Miscellaneous category.

Poor liquidity. You can't trade PPNs, at least not easily. Sometimes the underwriter commits to making "best efforts" to create a secondary market. But without an exchange listing, there is no guarantee of anything, and in a private, limited market the seller is usually at a profound disadvantage. Also, in some cases, if you sell within a certain period, an early trading charge will apply.

Profit limits. In some cases, the maximum return on a PPN is capped. However, you may have trouble figuring out exactly what the cap is because the language in the documentation supplied to investors is often vague on this point.

Complexity. The fundamentals of PPNs based on a well-known stock index are relatively easy to grasp. But it didn't take long for underwriters to create products that are far more complicated. First, they offered PPNs based on the performance of one or more mutual funds. Then they moved to baskets of stocks. Hedge funds aren't available to ordinary investors because of their high risk, but Bay Street got around that by packaging PPNs linked to hedge fund performance. Some PPNs are leveraged—if the underlying asset increases in value, you receive a return of 150 percent or 200 percent of the gain. We've now reached the point where you can buy PPNs that pay off if stocks go down! In June 2007, Jovian Capital launched Gibraltar Bear Canadian Banks Deposit Notes. The notes, with a three-and-a-half year term, gave investors a stake in a basket of shares in Canada's six largest banks. Usually, banks are regarded as one of the safest sectors in the stock market, but this PPN paid off only if the value of the shares in the portfolio dropped by the maturity date. Of course, that isn't impossible, but the odds are decidedly against it.

Tax surprises. If you make money on a PPN investment, your profits could be hit harder by taxes than you might expect if you hold the notes outside a registered plan. In some cases, the profit at maturity is taxed as interest at your full marginal rate and is not eligible for capital gains treatment. Make sure you understand all the tax implications of any PPN you consider.

Poor disclosure. The amount of information provided to investors interested in PPNs—or, more precisely, the lack of it—has been nothing short of disgraceful. Unlike mutual funds and new stock issues, no prospectus has been required (though steps are under way to change that). As PPNs grew more complex, the disclosure issue became even more pressing. In response, the Investment Dealers Association (IDA) in May 2007 issued a set of due diligence guidelines on PPN investing.[2] These are primarily for financial advisors, but the information they contain is useful for investors as well.

The lengthy IDA document praises PPNs for their flexibility, saying: "This enables the investor to enjoy risk-return characteristics which are not possible with other investments." But it then goes on to warn that "in order to enjoy these benefits, the investor must shoulder a number of risks," including inflation risk, credit risk, hedge counterparty risk, investment risk, timing risk, leverage risk, risk of reduced investment exposure, interest rate risk, and liquidity risk. As I read through this long list, I couldn't help but marvel at the number of risks involved in what is marketed as a "safe" investment. And that's not the end of it. The IDA also mentions several other areas of concern, including potential conflicts of interest, lack of transparency, fees and expenses, and tax uncertainty.

In fairness, the document is not a condemnation of PPNs but, rather, an attempt to educate advisors, and through them the public, about them. The IDA says these securities may be suitable for people who have a long time horizon and want exposure to the underlying asset without putting their principal at risk. My opinion is that there are better ways to keep risk low while earning decent returns. If you're thinking about putting money into a PPN, by all means read the IDA document, which will help in your evaluation. But before you go that route, consider the alternative suggestions that are explained in the next few chapters.

> **SLEEP-EASY ADVICE:** At first glance, PPNs may look like the perfect solution for a Sleep-Easy portfolio. In fact, they're very expensive and expose you to risks you probably never even considered. Avoid them.

Chapter 14

Do It *Your* Way

Lots of folks confuse bad management with destiny.
—Elbert Hubbard

There is a world of difference between the illusion and the reality of safety. In Chapter 13, I tried to convey the message that safety does not simply mean preservation of capital. Maintaining your financial status quo over several years actually means you are steadily losing purchasing power because of the effects of inflation.

Think of it in terms of a couple who retire on a fixed income of $3,000 a month. That may be enough to meet their expense needs now. But if inflation averages 2 percent annually over the next decade (the Bank of Canada's target rate), their income will buy only $2,451 worth of goods at the end of that time. They will have lost more than 18 percent of their purchasing power. At that point, they may be more than a little concerned about making ends meet.

That's why my Sleep-Easy approach to investing doesn't boil down to simply socking away your money in a savings account. If you're going to be truly comfortable with your finances, you want to know you're receiving a reasonable return on your investments.

That means finding the right balance—the perfect allocation of your resources to provide both a decent return and peace of mind.

There is one thing I want you to bear in mind: Our ultimate goal is *boredom*. If you're the type who loves the excitement of stock trading, this approach isn't for you. The whole point of this exercise is to eliminate the stress associated with money management. That means allocating your assets in a way that requires minimum maintenance on your part and frees your mind to concentrate on things you enjoy more.

So why not simply hand everything over to a professional money manager and let him or her do all the work? That might be a solution for some people, but I have seen too many cases in which clients fretted that their money was being mishandled and became angry and frustrated because they didn't know what to do about it. Here's one example from an email I received from a reader of one of my newsletters in late 2006:

> *I have had bad experiences with financial planners.*
> *Specifically, they are all over you for your business at the time of signing, however, they quickly forget about you after they make the initial sale. This has happened to me twice. The first time, I had invested $35,000 in technology before the tech bubble burst. I lost about $25,000 and the rep never called me once to offer changing my plan. The second time, I invested $10,000 in an RESP late in 2004. My report as of June 30, 2006, showed a total return of only $156.45.*

Clearly, this reader was upset—nothing Sleep-Easy about this situation. However, he had it in his power to switch course at any time. He could have taken control of the situation and given the advisor firm instructions to get out of the risky tech sector and move the money to more conservative securities. Instead, he remained passive—"the rep never called me once," he complains. The unanswered question is why he didn't pick up the phone himself. Instead, he sat by and watched his money go down the drain.

That's the problem with handing all the responsibility to someone else. If you don't pay attention to what's going on, you risk ending up in this type of situation. I've always said that no one cares about your money as much as you do. Don't ever forget it.

Sometimes the blunders of professional money managers are truly inexcusable. Several years ago, a friend asked me to look over her managed portfolios. She had two—one in an RRSP, the other in a taxable account. When I compared them, I was stunned to find that both accounts held exactly the same securities. No effort had been made to maximize tax efficiencies by placing interest-bearing securities in the registered plan and stocks and equity funds in the taxable account. As a result, she was paying more than $2,000 a year in unnecessary income tax. And for this, she was paying the managers an annual fee of well over $1,000. Needless to say, she fired them as soon as I pointed this out, but at that point she was out more than $10,000 in tax overpayments that could have been easily avoided.

This is not to say that having your money professionally managed is a bad thing. I know many people who are delighted with the service they get from their portfolio managers and wouldn't have it any other way. But in all cases, these people are actively involved in the process, reviewing their financial statements monthly, meeting with the manager at least twice a year, and giving new direction where appropriate.

If you see professional management as your ideal path to Sleep-Easy investing, then you should be prepared to do the same as my friends—stay involved. If that seems like too much trouble, or you don't have the knowledge needed to talk intelligently with a professional manager, then go a different route.

Recently, many people have chosen wrap accounts as their personal Sleep-Easy alternative. During the month of May 2007, most of the new money that was invested in mutual funds went into wraps—pre-packaged portfolios of individual funds. According to the Investment Funds Institute of Canada (IFIC), Canadians collectively poured $2.1 billion into wrap portfolios during that month, compared with only $1.4 billion invested in stand-alone funds. That gave wraps an astounding 60 percent market share. Wraps have become the fund industry's latest hot-ticket item. A fringe product only a few years ago, in mid-2007 they controlled over $106 billion in total assets. That was about 15 percent of IFIC's total mutual fund universe, and the market share is growing.

Clearly, investors like the convenience of this kind of one-stop shopping and the ability to invest in a portfolio that they expect will be tailored to their specific needs and risk tolerance. That wraps cost more in terms of a higher annual MER (on average you'll pay a premium of from 0.2 percent to 0.6 percent) doesn't seem to concern them.

But how good are these packages when it comes to your bottom-line returns? Although there are some exceptions, as a general rule you'll often do better by choosing a well-managed balanced fund and letting it go at that. But you can't easily quantify the difference.

Direct comparisons between the wraps offered by a company and its various balanced funds can be misleading because in many cases the asset mixes are different. For example, the AGF Elements Balanced Portfolio is made up of 13 AGF funds. In mid-2007, the asset mix was 63 percent equities and 37 percent fixed income, with a geographic mix that was 55 percent Canadian. Over the 12 months to May 31, the portfolio gained 13.3 percent. The AGF Canadian Balanced Fund had a slightly lower bonds/cash weighting at 33 percent and more domestic equity exposure. It was ahead 14.8 percent over the same period—a significant difference. I found a similar situation when I compared the AGF Elements Global Portfolio with the stand-alone AGF Global Equity Class.

The situation will differ from one company to the next, but the point to bear in mind is that wraps are not necessarily the best solution. If you like the concept, ask your financial advisor some hard questions before you decide to go ahead. Here are some of the most important ones.

What funds does it hold? A wrap is only as good as the funds it holds. If one or more of the funds in the portfolio is a chronic underperformer, it is likely that your overall return will be subpar.

What is the portfolio composition? Sometimes the name can be misleading. For instance, you may think that Mackenzie Financial's STAR Canadian Long-Term Growth Fund (now capped) is a pure domestic wrap on the basis of the name. Not so. Almost 30 percent of the portfolio is devoted to U.S. and foreign equity funds, such as Mackenzie Cundill Value Class and Mackenzie Universal U.S. Blue Chip Class.

What does it cost? Wraps usually have a higher MER than a comparable stand-alone fund. Find out what the premium is.

How has it performed? Most wraps are quite new, so they won't have much of a track record. All things being equal, try to find one that has been around for a few years so that you can compare its returns to those of a comparable stand-alone fund. For reasons explained above, you're unlikely to find a pure apples-to-apples comparison, but at least you can get some idea.

Is this portfolio the right fit for me? Typically, you will be given a form to complete that will contain questions ranging from your risk tolerance to your asset mix preference. Many people aren't knowledgeable enough to complete the form correctly and may therefore end up with a wrap that is unsuited to their needs. If you like the wrap concept, your best bet is to deal with an advisor who knows you personally and who understands where you're coming from. Otherwise, take time to properly assess your requirements before selecting a package.

The bottom line is that while wraps are hot sellers, there is no evidence that they produce better results than ordinary balanced funds, and selecting the right one to match your needs can be tricky. My suggestion is to create your own "wrap"—one that you know will be ideally suited to your personal Sleep-Easy approach.

Ever since I began writing about money, I have stressed proper asset allocation as the key to financial success. You'll find a chapter on the subject in every one of my investment books. I make no apology for that—if you get the allocation wrong, your results will almost certainly fall short of your expectations. So let's apply the fundamentals of asset allocation to the concept of Sleep-Easy investing.

Asset class selection is the most basic part of the process. There are four basic types of securities in every investment portfolio:

Cash. This consists of currency and highly liquid cash-equivalent securities such as Treasury bills, money market funds, high-interest savings accounts, and Canada Savings Bonds. Any asset that can quickly be converted to cash at its full face value qualifies.

Fixed income. These securities pay a specified (fixed) rate of return and have a maturity date, at which time your principal is returned. If they are sold or cashed in before that date, the result may be a loss or a penalty to the investor. Bonds, mortgages, fixed-rate preferred shares, and GICs fall into this asset class.

Variable income. In years past, this was not considered to be a separate asset class, but times and markets change. A variable-income security provides cash flow on a time-predictable basis (usually monthly or quarterly). However, the actual amount of the payment is not guaranteed and may vary considerably from one period to the next. These securities may or may not have maturity dates. Examples include floating-rate preferred shares, income-oriented mutual funds, and income trusts.

This may surprise some people, but I also include bond funds in this category. This is a departure from the past, as readers of my previous books will recognize, so a little explanation is in order.

In March 2007, I wrote an article in my *Internet Wealth Builder* newsletter about asset allocation. In response, I received an email from a White Rock, British Columbia, reader, as follows:

> *In that article you recommend iUnits CDN Bond Index Fund as a core fixed-income security for any portfolio. Although I have been investing for quite a few years I have not used ETFs [exchange-traded funds] to date. So perhaps my question just reflects my misconception as to how those securities perform. Over the past year, the security you recommend has traded as high as $29.69 and as low as $28. Over the past 30 days, the*

high has been $29.45 and the low $28.91. So it would appear that, depending on when one buys and sells, one could experience a capital gain or loss, or break even.

I have been under the impression that a defining feature of securities in the fixed-income category is the return of principal when held to maturity, e.g., bonds and GICs. Yet it would appear that return of principal is not guaranteed when using ETFs. If that is the case, why are they considered within the fixed-income category of securities rather than being classed as just another form of equity investing?

This question, which no one had ever asked me before, got me thinking, and it prompted me to go back and take a fresh look at the iShares fund, as well as other bond funds, both ETFs and mutual. My conclusion was that the reader was correct: They don't really fit the classic definition of a fixed-income security. The term "fixed income" indicates that the cash flow from the security—the income side of the equation—will always be the same and will not vary depending on the fortunes of the issuer. Of course, there are exceptions in cases where a bond issuer runs into financial difficulty and has to default, but if you stick with high-grade securities, that should never happen. It is also generally assumed that your principal is guaranteed when you invest in a fixed-income security, and that is in fact the case with GICs, Canada Savings Bonds, and government or corporate fixed-term bonds that are held until maturity, if the latter have been purchased at par.

However, mutual funds don't have a maturity date nor do most exchange-traded funds. They are like perpetual bonds, which have no set term. Since there is no maturity date, there is no guarantee you'll get back all your capital when you sell. As the reader pointed out, you can end up with a capital gain, a capital loss, or in a break-even position. If you want to increase the odds of a capital gain, you can buy bond funds when interest rates are high and expected to decline, but there are still no guarantees.

The unit value of all bond funds will fluctuate, albeit within a fairly narrow range, because the market prices of the securities held in the portfolio will move up or down, just as with stocks. Generally, when interest rates rise, the market price of a bond will fall, and the longer the term to maturity, the greater the effect. When rates fall, the opposite occurs.

It's also important to remember that when you invest in a bond fund of any type, you are buying a portfolio of securities. In the case of the iShares ETF, the portfolio always reflects the composition of the PCBond Universe Bond Index, so it will remain reasonably constant. Actively managed bond funds, such as those from a company like Phillips, Hager & North, are more dynamic. As bonds mature they of course will be replaced, but they may also be actively traded. The managers may decide that economic conditions require them to lengthen term (add more long-term issues) or shorten term (reduce longer-term exposure). They may see unusual opportunities and redeploy some of the assets. Any of these moves will change the mix.

Also, most bond funds don't really provide fixed income, in the sense that every payment you receive will be exactly the same. Your distributions may vary slightly depending on what is happening within the portfolio. For example, in 2006 the quarterly distributions from the iShares fund ranged from a low of $0.29093 per unit to a high of $0.32056. That's not a large range, but the payments were not exactly the same from quarter to quarter. So while the securities within the portfolio qualify as fixed income, the fund itself technically does not.

A bond fund offers the advantage of professional management and a diverse portfolio of government and corporate bonds, all wrapped up in a single purchase. But you sacrifice the guarantee of principal, and you have to expect minor variations in the payments. If that's a problem, stick with individual bonds or ask your broker to recommend a bond ladder to provide variation in maturities. Then you'll have a true fixed-income asset.

Growth. Assets in the growth category add value mainly through capital gains. Stocks and equity mutual funds are the most common examples. There are other elements to consider in the allocation process, but let's focus on the asset classes for now. For more insight, see Chapter 16.

Generally, the higher the percentage of cash and fixed-income securities in your portfolio, the less risky it will be. However, the trade-off is that your profit potential will be reduced as well. The more variable-income and growth securities you have, the greater the chance that you will achieve above-average returns. But you will also expose yourself to greater losses during periods when the stock market is in decline or when interest rates are moving sharply higher. You have to weigh these considerations and decide where you want to place your portfolio on the scale. If you choose to be ultra-conservative, you need to reconcile yourself to the fact that it will take longer to build your assets to whatever target level you have set. If you decide in favour of growth, you must be ready to accept the ups and downs of volatile stock and income trusts markets.

So the issue of risk management is central to the Sleep-Easy philosophy. You need to make the decisions necessary, either alone or in consultation with an advisor, to create a risk/return profile for your portfolio that you can comfortably live with for the foreseeable future. In the next two chapters, I'll show you exactly how to do this.

SLEEP-EASY ADVICE: Managed portfolios and wrap plans have become popular with people seeking a Sleep-Easy approach to their money. But the best course is to create a plan that is precisely tailored to your personal situation.

Chapter 15

Choose Your Partners

Riches amassed in haste will diminish, but those collected by little and little will multiply.

—Goethe

So much of our success and happiness in life depends on choosing the right partner, whether in marriage or in business. The analogy can be extended to your investments. In this case, your partners are the securities you choose. If you make poor selections, they'll make you miserable. If you choose wisely and well, they'll provide financial security. That in itself won't make you happy, but it will certainly help. As the great Broadway singer Sophie Tucker once said: "I've been rich and I've been poor. Believe me honey, rich is better."

If all the potential "partners" for your money stood in a line, it would extend around the block and down the street. But most of them are totally unsuited for inclusion in a Sleep-Easy portfolio.

Take that guy over there, the one who keeps jumping around. That's Mr. Commodity Futures. He has a reputation for being erratic and unstable. Tell him to go home.

See that demure young lady by the window? Meet Ms. PPN. Her voice is soft and reassuring, but beneath that languid exterior she's iron-tough and she comes with a hefty price tag. Say goodbye.

Then there's the fellow at the back who keeps clicking a pair of dice while he talks incessantly to the man beside him. He's Mr. Penny Stock. They say he's living on pure oxygen and could keel over at any time. He's not someone you want to be involved with.

In fact, you can send the majority of the candidates packing. There are only a handful of securities that are worthy of consideration as your partners in a Sleep-Easy portfolio. Let me introduce them.

Suitable Partners

High-interest savings accounts. After years of offering a pittance for your money, banks and other financial institutions are back competing for a share of your savings by providing high-interest savings accounts. Almost all are protected by some form of deposit insurance, but before you sign on, verify with the company exactly what the coverage is.

Government savings bonds. We're most familiar with Canada Savings Bonds, but many provinces now offer their own issues, which come with a higher yield. If savings bonds are on your list, the provincials are a better bet, but they are available only for a limited time each year.

Treasury bills. You won't find anything much safer than Treasury bills. They're short-term notes (maturities of not more than one year) issued and guaranteed by governments. Because they're secure, they pay a low rate of interest, but they're a good place to park money for the short term.

Bankers' acceptances. These are also short-term notes, but they're issued by banks. As a result, they are seen as having slightly more risk so the interest they pay is a little higher.

Money market mutual funds. When you choose one of these funds, you're buying a portfolio of Treasury bills, bankers' acceptances, and similar short-term notes. They have always been regarded as very safe; however, a few have lost small amounts of money during sudden, sharp upward interest rate spikes, usually in the form of skipped interest payments.

However, the safety of these funds was called into question in August 2007 when it was revealed that a number of them had invested in asset-backed securities based on U.S. subprime mortgages. When the subprime mortgage market collapsed, the value of these assets was undermined. Fund sponsors were forced to step in and bail out investors; one of these was the National Bank of Canada, which bought back $1.85 billion worth of asset-backed notes from its own money market funds and those of subsidiary Altamira Investment Services.

Concern about the possible risk to money market funds prompted some companies, such as Vancouver-based Phillips, Hager & North, to issue press releases stating they had no exposure to the subprime market and invested only in top-quality assets.

Although no fund investor lost money, the credibility of money funds as safe havens was tarnished to some extent. Anyone who is at all concerned should stick with funds that invest only in securities issued or guaranteed by governments. These are called T-bill funds, and all the major banks offer them.

Guaranteed investment certificates/term deposits. For years,
GICs formed the bedrock of most conservative investment portfolios. But when interest rates started a long decline after peaking
in the early 1980s, investors switched to alternatives. Returns
improved in 2007, but GIC rates are still relatively unattractive,
particularly the GIC rates from the major banks. Because the interest is heavily taxed, GICs are best confined to registered plans.

Avoid market-linked GICs of any kind for reasons explained in
Chapter 13.

Bonds. Not all bonds are created equal. Don't ever forget that.
Bonds are candidates for your Sleep-Easy portfolio, but only if you
choose correctly. Short- to mid-term government bonds are the
best choice for this purpose. Long-term bonds (maturities of more
than 10 years) can be extremely volatile when interest rates are on
the move. The rule is: The shorter the term, the less the risk. Avoid
high-yield ("junk") bonds.

Stripped bonds. These are bonds from which the interest portion
has been removed and sold separately as stripped coupons. You buy
only the face value of the bond, for which you pay a discounted
price. When the bond matures, you collect the principal. The
difference between what you paid and the amount you receive
amounts to the "interest" you earned.

Strips, as they are known for short, can be extremely volatile, so
I don't recommend them if you may have to sell before maturity.
But if you're looking for a guaranteed return at the end of the day,
they're a good choice. They should be held only in an RRSP
because the tax implications of keeping them in a non-registered
account are onerous, and they are unsuitable for RRIFs because
they provide no cash flow. Choose only government strips for

safety. A few years ago, some brokerage firms stripped long-term Bell Canada bonds, in some cases with maturities 30 years out, and sold them at huge discounts to their clients. At the time, Bell bonds were considered to be among the elite of corporate issues and were highly rated by agencies such as Standard & Poor's. Then came the massive leveraged buyout of BCE Incorporated in mid-2007. At the time of writing, it appeared that Bell bonds would be relegated to junk status, and prices had tumbled dramatically. A strip that had seemed to be rock-solid at the time of purchase had become a drag on returns.

Bond funds. Most bond funds are broadly diversified, though there are several subcategories that specialize in certain types of fixed-income securities. These include short-term bonds, foreign bonds, and high-yield bonds. As I pointed out in the previous chapter, bond funds do not guarantee a specific rate of return, nor do they have a set maturity date. They also are more expensive than buying the bonds yourself because of sales commissions and MERs. But some investors prefer them for the convenience they provide.

Income from bond funds is received almost exclusively in the form of interest, which is fully taxable outside a registered plan. Therefore, if at all possible you should keep your bond funds in an RRSP, RRIF, or similar plan. The frequency of distributions varies, so check before deciding. Most pay either monthly or quarterly, but a few make distributions only once a year. If steady cash flow is a prime concern, a fund such as that wouldn't be appropriate.

Mortgage-backed securities. These are known in the industry as MBS. They are fixed-income securities that invest in a pool of residential first mortgages. Those that are insured under the National

Housing Act (NHA) are safe, as they are unconditionally guaranteed by Canada Mortgage and Housing Corporation. However, returns can be very low, especially when interest rates are down. Avoid MBS offerings that are not NHA insured; the subprime mortgage crisis that blew up in the United States in 2007 underlined the risk of investing in low-quality mortgage pools.

Mortgage funds. There are not many pure mortgage mutual funds left any more, and they have been out of favour with investors because of their low returns. But from a safety perspective they rank near the top of the pyramid. Not a single mortgage mutual fund has recorded a calendar year loss in this century.

Fixed-income exchange-traded funds (ETFs). If you are investing for the long term, ETFs are a cheaper way than mutual funds to hold bonds. Unlike no-load mutual funds, you have to pay a sales commission upfront, since ETFs are traded on the Toronto Stock Exchange. But after that, the annual costs, as expressed in the fund's management expense ratio (MER), are much lower than you'd pay for a bond mutual fund. For example, the most popular Canadian fixed-income ETF is the iShares CDN Bond Index Fund, which trades on the TSX under the symbol XBB. It tracks the performance of the PC Bond Universe Index (formerly known as the Scotia Capital Universe Bond Index), which is a basket of securities that represents the entire range of the Canadian bond market. The MER on this fund is only 0.3 percent. By comparison, the popular TD Canadian Bond Fund has a 1.39 percent MER, more than one percentage point higher. That charge comes right off your bottom line: The TD fund posted a three-year average annual compound rate of return of 4.14 percent to June 30, 2007, while the iShares units gained an average of 5.28 percent a year over the same period. Both funds track the same index, so the difference is almost entirely due to the TD fund's higher MER.

Preferred shares. I include preferred shares on this list with some trepidation. They're attractive because they are usually (but not always) stable in price, their distributions are reasonably predictable, and they are eligible for the dividend tax credit, which makes them very effective in non-registered accounts.

The problem is that they come with all kinds of small print that sometimes catches even professional money managers by surprise. The most common problem is redemption clauses that allow the issuer to buy back the preferreds at specific times for predetermined prices. For example, the Enbridge Series A preferreds pay a dividend of 5.5 percent, which looks attractive when you take into account the tax credit. But the company can redeem the entire issue on 30 days' notice at any time for a price of $25. Anyone who pays more than that risks incurring a capital loss if Enbridge triggers the redemption clause.

My company once suffered the embarrassment of recommending a high-quality preferred in one of its newsletters, only to have that company unexpectedly announce it was calling the issue just a few days later. That sort of thing can happen at any time, so if you are going to include preferreds in your portfolio, make sure you find out all the terms and conditions attached to an issue before buying.

Another type of problem can arise if there is a major change in corporate status. When BCE Incorporated went on the sales block early in 2007, the price of Bell and BCE preferred shares plummeted because of concerns that the company's credit rating would be downgraded. Needless to say, investors were not pleased.

I wish I could tell you that you could get around this by investing in preferred shares through a mutual fund, but I can't. Most of the so-called dividend funds on offer have few, if any, preferreds in their asset mix. Among the rare exceptions are the GGOF Monthly Dividend Fund, which at the time of writing was closed to new investors, and the Signature Dividend Fund, offered by CI Investments. And in both cases, preferreds accounted for less than half the total assets.

The only pure preferred share fund that I know of in Canada is the Diversified Preferred Share Trust. It is managed by Sentry Select and trades on the Toronto Stock Exchange under the symbol DPS.UN. It is worth considering if you want to add a preferred share component to your portfolio without going through the hassle of picking the issues yourself.

Selected income funds. Many investors have turned to income-oriented mutual funds in recent years for the cash flow they provide. Several of these funds include the words "monthly income" in their names. As you might expect, they offer steady monthly payments, often at a fixed amount per unit. But the distributions are not guaranteed and can be changed at any time.

Income funds are useful additions to a Sleep-Easy portfolio, but use care in deciding which ones to choose. The assets in these funds typically include a mix of Canadian and foreign common stocks, income trusts, bonds, and Treasury bills. Some are more aggressively managed than others and are therefore more vulnerable to loss when markets turn down. My advice is to focus on funds that take a conservative approach and that have a track record of holding up well in tough times. One of the best performers in this context has been the TD Monthly Income Fund, which came through the 2000–02 bear market without suffering a loss in any calendar year. In fact, its worst performance was a 9.47 percent gain in 2002. Other funds of this type that came through the bear market unscathed were the BMO Monthly Income Fund, the RBC Monthly Income Fund, and the CIBC Monthly Income Fund.

Conservative equity funds. You need a growth component in your Sleep-Easy portfolio, but you want something that will minimize risk. By all means consider an equity mutual fund but, as with the income funds, pick one with a record of beating bear markets. That means focusing on value-style funds run by managers who place preservation of capital at the top of their priority list.

One example of such a manager is Francis Chou, who was named Canada's "manager of the decade" by the fund industry a few years ago. He is a dedicated value manager who absolutely refuses to overpay for a stock. If that means sitting in cash for a while, so be it—better that than to fritter away clients' money. Back in the late 1990s, Chou launched a broadside at investors and managers who were paying absurd prices for tech stocks in the hope they could turn around and sell them for even more absurd prices. He stayed on the sidelines, biding his time, all the while accepting criticism for his funds' lacklustre showing. Then came the tech crash, and Chou's warnings were borne out. His funds prospered. The Chou RRSP Fund posted calendar-year gains of 16.5 percent, 17 percent, and 31.9 percent over the three years from 2000 to the end of 2002, at a time when most equity funds were bleeding red ink. His Chou Associates Fund, which has more of a U.S. and international focus, did almost as well, with gains of 8.4 percent, 21.4 percent, and 30 percent.

Chou's style is somewhat unorthodox, however, and not to everyone's taste. For a mainstream bear-beating manager, consider Kim Shannon, who now manages several funds within the Brandes group. Previously, she ran the CI Canadian Investment Fund for several years, where she established a reputation as a smart, disciplined manager who knew how to protect assets in rough times. That fund never lost money in a calendar year under her direction; its worst performance was a break-even finish in 2002. Other managers who are known for their conservative approach to stock selection include Gerald Coleman and Eric Bushell of CI Investments, Jerry Javasky and Peter Cundill of Mackenzie Financial, and Larry Sarbit, who runs his own fund family.

Some dividend funds also qualify for mention here. Most funds of this type are really nothing more than blue chip stock funds and could just as easily be slotted into the Canadian Equity category. Among the funds in this group that came through the bear market without a losing calendar year are Dynamic Dividend Fund, the previously mentioned GGOF Monthly Dividend Fund, the IA Clarington Dividend Income Fund, and the Mavrix Dividend and Income Fund (which was helped by a large income trust component). The RBC Canadian Dividend Fund was a near-miss, with a 0.48 percent loss in 2002 the only blemish on its record.

Low-risk balanced funds. This group is a real dog's breakfast. Balanced funds may invest in any combination of bonds, mortgages, income trusts, dividend-paying stocks, and preferred shares. So you need to be very careful in your selections. For Sleep-Easy purposes, low-risk funds are the best choices, but these are often difficult to identify because they rank well down on the returns scale. One example is the Mackenzie Sentinel Income Fund, which holds about 60 percent of its assets in bonds and cash, thus giving it a very low level of volatility. How low? The worst 12-month period in the entire history of this fund, which goes back to 1974, was a 0.08 percent loss (B units) over the year ending in February 1999. Think about that. This is a fund that is well over 30 years old and the worst investors have ever done over a year was a loss of less than one-tenth of 1 percent. It's a perfect candidate for a Sleep-Easy portfolio. Granted, the returns aren't exciting, but an average annual gain of 7.49 percent over five years (to June 30, 2007) is more than acceptable given the low risk you incur.

Real estate investment trusts (REITs). These are the only income trusts that have been exempted from the new trust tax. They are also the most stable category. That does not mean they are without risk—they are vulnerable to interest rate movements, and a collapse in the real estate sector, such as we experienced back in the 1980s, would knock them for a loop. But the degree of risk is acceptable for our purposes in view of the good tax-advantaged cash flow these funds offer, their growth potential, and their consistency. You can choose individual REITs or invest in a fund that specializes in them, such as the Sentry Select REIT Fund or the iShares CDN REIT Sector Index Fund, which trades on the Toronto Stock Exchange under the symbol XRE.

The Wallflowers

You will probably have noticed that I have not included several types of popular securities on my list. They have been left off deliberately because I do not believe they are compatible with a true Sleep-Easy approach to money management. Here are some of the partners that you should leave to dance with someone else.

Common stocks. While certain types of equity funds are on our partners list, common stocks themselves are not. That's because they require more intensive management, which is not what Sleep-Easy investing is about. And even the bluest of the blue chips can experience significant losses at times. When the news broke in July 2005 that Canadian Imperial Bank of Commerce had reached a US$2.4 billion out-of-court settlement with Enron shareholders, the stock price plummeted by more than $10 a share, a loss of close to 14 percent. That was almost unheard-of among Canada's big five banks. It turned out to be a terrific buying opportunity. Gavin Graham of Guardian Group of Funds (GGOF) and contributing editor to my *Income Investor* newsletter recommended the stock to readers in August of that year when it was trading at $69.05 and many skittish investors had departed the scene, in some cases selling at a loss. By early 2007 it was back over $100 a share.

CIBC isn't an isolated case. Many other supposedly blue chip stocks have been savaged over the years, including Bombardier, Stelco, Royal Trust, Air Canada, and Nortel. So leave the stock trading to your fund managers.

Income trusts. With the exception of REITs, trusts should also be excluded from your portfolio. Although the yields are still attractive, there is too much uncertainty surrounding trusts to make them worthy partners for a true Sleep-Easy investor. With the new trust tax set to come into effect in 2011, the sector is in turmoil. Over the next couple of years, we are going to see more takeovers, mergers, privatizations, and corporate conversions as the trusts look for a way out of the box the Conservative government placed them in. It is impossible to predict what the ultimate effect will be on the share price of any given trust or on the distributions paid to unitholders.

Most ETFs. Although I have included bond ETFs and one REIT ETF on the partners list, I suggest you avoid all the others. Some readers may be surprised by this, as ETFs have been widely touted as the simplest way to invest and form the backbone of many so-called couch potato portfolios.

But there are two major problems with ETFs when it comes to a Sleep-Easy approach. The first is that they are designed to track the performance of an underlying benchmark index, for good or for bad. ETFs are passive securities: The managers have no discretion to intervene in order to diminish risk during market downturns. The portfolio must always reflect the composition of the benchmark index. Over the long term, studies show that the approach works. But it requires a great deal of self-discipline to stick with an index fund when the stock markets go into a prolonged dive and there's doom and gloom everywhere. Investors in the National Bank Canadian Index Fund suffered a 15.48 percent loss in 2001, followed by another 14.83 percent decline in 2002. At the end of it all, for every $1,000 they had invested at the start of 2001, they had less than $720 left two years later. Many people would have bolted by that point, thus defeating the basic strategy of owning ETFs. Those who remained were probably experiencing a lot of restless nights wondering if stocks were ever going to turn around. Again, that's not what Sleep-Easy investing is all about.

The second problem stems from the booming popularity of ETFs. The whole concept of investing simplicity has been twisted out of shape, and we now have ETFs that are almost as high-risk as penny stocks. Some of these focus on obscure indexes that they have actually created themselves to justify their existence. These pseudo-ETFs have become big business in the United States and are now making their way into Canada.

One example of what's happening in the United States is the lineup of HealthShares ETFs, launched early in 2007. The funds are based on such obscure benchmarks as the "Metabolic-

Endocrine Disorders Index," the "Autoimmune-Inflammation Index," the "GI/Gender Health Index," and the "Ophthalmology Index." What exactly are these indexes? They're the brain-children of XShares Group LLC, which promotes and distributes the funds. The only reason for these so-called indexes to exist is to legitimize the HealthShares funds as ETFs. Otherwise, they would simply be closed-end funds, without the cachet and consumer acceptance that the ETF label brings with it.

This is just the tip of a very large and growing iceberg. An article by Marc Hogan titled "The Weird World of ETFs," published in the February 2007 issue of *BusinessWeek,* cautioned that ETFs "now provide exposure to even the narrowest—and sometimes most outlandish—investment niches." As examples, the article cited new ETFs based on everything from carbon emission credits to nanotechnology.

I see all kinds of problems with this disquieting trend from the Sleep-Easy investor's perspective. The first and most obvious one is that there is no real track record on which to base an investment decision. Sponsors of this new breed of ETF claim that they carefully back-test the artificial indexes they create, but who knows what assumptions go into those calculations.

Another concern is that history shows that the narrower the base of any kind of fund, the riskier it is. By creating ETFs based on market segments that are so small only a few stocks can fit in (many of them being small or micro-cap issues), the industry is building a much higher potential for loss into its products than many people may realize. The HealthShares website includes this specific warning to potential investors: "HealthShares™ are not actively managed and are subject to risks similar to stocks, including those related to short selling and margin maintenance. HealthShares™ ETFs are subject to increased risks associated with investing in a specific sector compared to more a diversified investment."[1] That should be enough to scare off any Sleep-Easy investor.

In another twist, we now have ETFs that pay off when the benchmark index goes *down*—shorting the market made easy, if you like. Some of these are even leveraged, so that for every point an index drops, you get double the return. Of course, as we saw in Chapter 9 on leveraging, it works both ways—if markets rise, you lose double. There are legitimate ways to use these bear ETFs as a form of portfolio insurance to protect profits in the event of a market downturn, but I doubt most people will treat them like that. Instead, I suspect they'll be used as a means of trying to outguess the market, with potentially disastrous results.

Finally, there is the issue of cost. One of the big attractions of ETFs is that they're supposedly cheap to own once you've paid the brokerage commission to acquire them. The iShares CDN Large Cap Index Fund (TSX: XIU), which tracks the S&P/TSX 60 Index, has an MER of 0.17 percent. In contrast, the published fees for the HealthShares products are 1.09 percent, much higher than you would pay for an ETF based on a recognized index.

Precious metals. At some point, you will almost certainly be tempted to respond to the siren call of the gold bugs to invest money in bullion or precious metals mutual funds. Ever since I started in this business more than 25 years ago, I have listened to gold experts explain why it was inevitable that the price of the yellow metal would soon rise to $1,000 and beyond. It hasn't happened yet. In fact, gold is extremely volatile and has no place in a low-risk portfolio, despite what you may hear elsewhere. As recently as 2004, almost all precious metals funds sold in Canada incurred double-digit losses, in some cases in excess of 20 percent. Sorry, that's not for us.

SLEEP-EASY ADVICE: Choose your securities from those included on my Sleep-Easy partners list and ignore everything else. You'll be able to build a solid portfolio with them, one that combines a high degree of safety with a respectable return.

Chapter 16

Balancing Act

The reasonable man adapts himself to the world.
—George Bernard Shaw

I find Chinese restaurant menus frustrating. There are dozens of items from which to choose, and I don't have a clue what some of them are. They may be delicious, but I tend to avoid them for fear I'll end up with something I consider to be inedible. It can happen. Once when my wife and I were visiting San Francisco, we went to an internationally famous restaurant that was highly praised for its dim sum. Waiters moved among the tables with large carts, each of which held three covered serving dishes. We noticed that only some of the carts were brought to our table. Many passed by, stopping only at tables where the diners were Chinese.

I called to the waiter who was pushing one of those carts and motioned him over. After all, we were in San Francisco's Chinatown, and we wanted to experience the best it had to offer. The waiter shook his head, but I insisted. Finally, he reluctantly brought the cart over. He didn't speak much English, so I pointed to one of the covered dishes and indicated we wanted some of whatever was inside. He frowned and tried once again to say no, but I pointed more vigorously. Finally, he removed the cover and we found ourselves staring at a bowl filled with steamed chicken feet. Scrawny, yellow, and, to us, decidedly unappetizing chicken feet. He moved to pile some on my plate, at which point I shook my head vigorously and motioned him away. With a shrug and just the hint of a smile, he replaced the lid and moved off to another table. That's why, to this day, my wife and I hesitate to order unknown dishes from Chinese menus.

I'm telling this story because in the last chapter I set out a lengthy list of menu items for possible inclusion in a Sleep-Easy investment portfolio. Some of those items may not be familiar to you, and you may hesitate to try them as a result. Fair enough. You don't need to use all of them; in fact, some of the choices will be unsuitable in certain situations. What you must decide is which ones you *do* want to include and the weighting to give each in your portfolio.

Before you begin choosing from my menu, you must prepare a master plan for asset allocation. Most investors are more concerned with trying to pick individual securities than they are with ensuring that their asset mix is right for their goals and temperament. That's putting the cart before the horse. Asset allocation should be the first step. Once you know how you want to structure your portfolio, you can concentrate on selecting the best securities. But put first things first. Proper asset allocation is the cornerstone of smart investing. Repeated studies have shown that having the right mix is more important to your total return than the individual securities you choose.

Yet even seasoned investors lose track of their portfolio balance from time to time, especially when markets are volatile. Part of the problem goes back to human nature. When stock markets are performing well, there is a natural tendency to direct more of your money toward equities. Steady profits produce a sort of investor euphoria, a state that leads to impaired judgment. That lasts until the moment the market turns around. Then people rush to make changes—perhaps too late, depending on the speed and severity of the slide.

Remember 2000? At the start of the year, investors were giddy. The high-tech boom was making instant millionaires out of thousands of people, the Dow was setting new records, and many pundits were telling us that we were experiencing a new paradigm that would see stocks continue to rise for the next decade. By Easter, the markets were in full retreat, and we all know what came next. By autumn, we were into a full-blown bear market that was to last more than two years.

That period provides a dramatic illustration of the impact that asset allocation has on an investment portfolio and how you can use this information to your advantage. Using a computer program developed by Ativa Interactive of Hamilton, Ontario, I looked at the effect of different asset mixes on a portfolio during the period from August 2000 to September 2002, when the bear market was in full control. A portfolio that was 80 percent in equities (our growth category) and 20 percent in bonds (fixed income) would have lost almost 31 percent during that period. A portfolio with a 50–50 weighting would have been down about 12 percent. With a 60–40 weighting in favour of bonds, the loss was trimmed to less than 6 percent. At a 30–70 stocks to bonds ratio, the portfolio actually turned a small profit over the period. That's the power of asset allocation at work.

So don't procrastinate. If you've been telling yourself for some time that you really need to sit down and revise your portfolio, do it now. It's a perfect opportunity to set a new direction based on a clear and consistent investment philosophy.

Now let's get down to specifics. How much emphasis should you give each of the four asset groups in your portfolio? As you'll recall from Chapter 14, the categories are cash, fixed income, variable income, and growth. There are several factors to consider, including your age, your time horizon, your tax situation (if it is a non-registered portfolio), the economic climate, your risk tolerance, and so on.

As we saw in Chapter 7, all securities have their own risk/return profile, even those within the same asset class. For example, a U.S.-dollar money market fund has to be considered to be higher risk than a Canadian-dollar money market fund because it introduces an additional variable: currency fluctuation. Of course, that also means that the reward potential of the U.S. dollar fund is higher, since the assets in it will be worth more if the loonie declines. So risk management is a key element in allocating your assets in accordance with your safety-versus-profits priorities.

In addition to asset class selection and risk, a well-planned portfolio mix will also take into account geographic distribution and style diversification. Here is a brief overview of each.

Geographic Distribution

There is a natural tendency to favour Canadian securities because they are familiar. However, it is easy to overdo this, to your detriment. Many studies have been conducted of what is known as the *efficient frontier*. This is a portfolio analysis technique that seeks to identify the point on a graph at which the blended domestic and foreign content attains maximum reward potential consistent with minimal risk. Although the numbers vary, the results almost always suggest that non-Canadian securities should make up between 40 and 60 percent of your total mix. If that seems high, remember that Canada represents only 2 to 3 percent of the world's equity markets. We are a bit player on the international stage, and we have relatively few multinational companies. Most of what we consider to be corporate giants, like the big banks, are pipsqueaks when measured against foreign competitors in the same field.

There are four main areas of the globe to consider:

- *Canada.* The majority of your securities should be in your home country and your home currency.
- *United States.* The number one economic power in the world should be strongly represented in all portfolios.
- *Europe.* The euro has been very strong in recent years, and European markets have outperformed expectations, so this continent should also be represented in your mix.
- *Pacific Rim.* China is rapidly emerging as one of the world's leading manufacturing countries, while India is a growing hotbed for technology. Japan continues to be a potent economic force, despite the fact that its stock market has languished for years. The growth potential in this part of the world is huge, but the risks are also high.

Style Diversification

Professional money managers use one of several styles to select securities. For our purposes, let's keep things simple and focus on the three most basic ones:

- *Value.* This approach looks for securities that are relatively cheap by using traditional measures such as price to book value and price/earnings ratio. This is a tried-and-true formula for achieving long-term success, and many of the world's greatest investors, including Warren Buffett and Sir John Templeton, use these techniques. But its effectiveness is cyclical. Value investors tend to underperform in red-hot markets such as those of the late 1990s and the 2003–07 period. But they excel in protecting capital when markets are weak, as in the bear market of 2000–02.

- *Growth.* In this case, the emphasis is on finding stocks of companies that have the potential to grow more rapidly than their competitors. Strong increases in revenue and market share assume greater importance in the valuation process than price/earnings ratios. Good growth managers consistently outperform in bull markets.

- *Indexing.* The goal of these funds is to emulate the performance of an underlying benchmark index, such as the S&P/TSX Composite, less expenses.

Some people prefer to use a pure indexing approach. However, I favour a more active style because I feel that many investors will decide to bail out of stock market-based index securities during a bear period as losses mount up. Between 2000 and 2002, the TD Japanese Index Fund suffered back-to-back losses of 26.6 percent, 26.1 percent, and 11.6 percent. I wonder how many folks would have stuck it out the whole time.

That's why I suggest you ensure your portfolio includes both value and growth securities in the variable income and equity sections. You can achieve this through individual securities selection; however, that will require a fair amount of analysis on your part or on the part of your financial advisor. It may be simpler to select equity and variable income mutual funds that adopt each approach.

To reduce the problem to its most basic, let's assume that the entire Canadian equity portion of your portfolio is to be held in just two mutual funds. To implement style diversification in this situation, you want to be sure that one fund is managed according to firm value principles, while the other is run on a growth-oriented basis.

Keep in mind that there is no such thing as a one-size-fits-all asset mix. You need to tailor your formula to your specific objectives and risk-tolerance level. Sleep-Easy investors should always err on the side of caution. There is nothing wrong with giving up a little profit potential when the trade-off is better protection of your capital.

As a broad guideline, the basic allocation for a balanced portfolio would be 50 percent equities, 25 percent fixed income, 15 percent variable income, and 10 percent cash. Using those figures as a base, let's look at some sample portfolio profiles.

An RRSP portfolio. You should never be overly aggressive in an RRSP portfolio, no matter what your age. This is your personal pension plan, and it should be invested accordingly, with capital preservation as a high priority. Because we're applying a Sleep-Easy approach throughout, I suggest limiting your equities weighting to a maximum of 40 percent instead of the 50 percent maximum in a standard balanced portfolio. Half of that should be in Canada, with the other half invested in the United States and overseas. Fixed-income securities should account for 25 to 35 percent of the mix, with variable-income securities at 15 to 20 percent and the rest in cash. Because we're dealing with a registered plan, interest-bearing securities may form a large part of the mix.

Choosing from the menu in Chapter 15, here is what a Sleep-Easy RRSP portfolio might look like. Note that this is a basic portfolio; mix and match any appropriate securities from my list as you wish. The estimated returns are annual averages over 10 years. Year-to-year returns may vary considerably from these numbers but, based on historical results, they are reasonable over the long term.

Basic Sleep-Easy RRSP Portfolio

Type of Security	Asset Class	Weighting (%)	Estimated Annual Return (%)
Money market fund or high-interest account	Cash	5	3.5
GICs	Fixed income	15	4.5
Stripped bonds	Fixed income	20	5
Bond funds or fixed-income ETFs	Variable income	10	5
Conservative income funds	Variable income	10	7
Conservative Canadian equity funds	Growth	20	8
Conservative foreign equity funds	Growth	20	8
Total/average		100	6.25

When you choose specific securities, especially in the growth category, focus on mutual funds with a proven track record of protecting capital during a bear market. There is no guarantee they won't experience some loss in a future market downturn, but any decline in net asset value should be minimal and they will snap back quickly.

For your variable-income bond fund, the iShares CDN Bond Index Fund that I mentioned in Chapter 15 is a good core holding and is especially useful for investors who don't have adequate resources to properly diversify their bond weighting.

Your stripped bonds should be confined to government issues. You'll get a slightly better return from provincial government strips than from those based on Canada bonds.

A RRIF/LIF portfolio. Here the twin emphases are capital preservation and cash flow. Since most people with RRIFs and LIFs are 65 and older, care must be used to create an asset mix that will minimize the chance of serious loss. That means a greater emphasis on income securities and a correspondingly lower percentage of equities. A low-risk RRIF portfolio should not have more than about 30 percent exposure to the stock market. The fixed-income segment should be around 35 percent, with the variable-income portion at 25 percent. There should be about 10 percent in cash to fund the periodic withdrawals.

Basic Sleep-Easy RRIF/LIF Portfolio

Type of Security	Asset Class	Weighting (%)	Estimated Annual Return (%)
Money market fund or high-interest account	Cash	10	3.5
GICs	Fixed income	15	4.5
Investment-grade bonds	Fixed income	20	5
Bond funds or fixed-income ETFs	Variable income	10	5
Conservative income funds	Variable income	15	7
Conservative Canadian equity funds	Growth	15	8
Conservative foreign equity funds	Growth	15	8
Total/average		100	5.98

The main problem with this mix is that from age 71 onward, it won't generate enough cash flow to meet the minimum withdrawal requirements. Under the current formula, a person who is 71 years old must withdraw during the next 12 months at least 7.38 percent of the plan's total value on January 1 of the year in question. The percentage gradually increases each year thereafter. For example, a 71-year-old with a RRIF worth $100,000 on January 1 would need to take out at least $7,380 by December 31 of that year. But the Sleep-Easy RRIF portfolio will generate only an estimated $5,980, leaving a shortfall of $1,400.

This leaves the investor with two choices: take more risk to increase yield or allow the gradual erosion of the capital base through withdrawals. Neither is an ideal option for a Sleep-Easy investor, and I have contended for many years that the federal government should revert to its pre-1993 withdrawal scale, which was much less onerous up to age 77. Failing that, my advice for those who find their withdrawals running ahead of their returns is to adjust the asset mix a little without adding undue risk. Here's how it might be done.

Adjusted Sleep-Easy RRIF/LIF Portfolio

Type of Security	Asset Class	Weighting (%)	Estimated Annual Return (%)
Money market fund or high-interest account	Cash	7.5	3.5
GICs	Fixed income	10	4.5
Investment-grade bonds	Fixed income	17.5	5
Bond funds or fixed-income ETFs	Variable income	10	5
Conservative income funds	Variable income	25	7
Conservative Canadian equity funds	Growth	15	8
Conservative foreign equity funds	Growth	15	8
Total/average		100	6.24

The changes have enabled us to squeeze an additional quarter-point of return out of the portfolio without unduly compromising ourselves on the risk side of the ledger. We're still short of the minimum withdrawal required at age 71, but we have reduced the deficit to $1,140. To cut it further, still more risk would have to be added.

I suggest using a conservative approach at the outset. If you set up your RRIF/LIF at age 65, choose my suggested basic portfolio to begin with (or something close to it) and see what happens over the next few years. If my estimates are anywhere near the actual returns you receive, the profits will more than offset the minimum payment requirements until you reach age 71. If during that period you hit a strong stock market run (which is likely), the return on your equity funds could be well in excess of my projected 8 percent. For example, over the three years to June 30, 2007, the average pure Canadian equity fund added 17.7 percent annually. If you are fortunate enough to experience a run like that, you'll have a nice cushion in your RRIF/LIF when the maximum withdrawal requirement passes the 7 percent mark.

A non-registered portfolio (under age 50). An additional variable has to be taken into account when constructing a Sleep-Easy non-registered portfolio: taxes. Your goal should be to maximize growth at reasonable risk, while paying as little of the profit as is legally possible to governments. That means minimizing holdings of interest-bearing securities such as bonds, bond funds, mortgage-backed securities, and GICs.

For this type of portfolio, low-risk equity mutual funds can be given a weighting of up to 50 percent. Fixed-income securities are kept at a minimum (15 percent) because of the tax implications. Give more priority to variable-income selections with tax advantages (30 percent). Cash should be minimal.

Here's what a basic Sleep-Easy non-registered portfolio for a younger person might look like:

Basic Sleep-Easy Non-Registered Portfolio (under age 50)

Type of Security	Asset Class	Weighting (%)	Estimated Annual Return (%)
Money market fund or high-interest account	Cash	5	3.5
Investment-grade bonds	Fixed income	15	5
Preferred shares or funds	Variable income	10	5.5
REITs	Variable income	10	7
Conservative income funds	Variable income	10	7
Conservative Canadian equity funds	Growth	25	8
Conservative foreign equity funds	Growth	25	8
Total/average		100	6.97

This gives us a very tax-efficient portfolio. The average annual return may seem modest at just below 7 percent, but remember that a large part of that gain will be taxed at low rates.

One way to reduce the tax hit on the bonds in this portfolio is to hold them in a low-risk balanced fund. To illustrate, the Mackenzie Sentinel Income Fund, mentioned in Chapter 15, invests about 60 percent of its assets in bonds and cash. However, in 2006 only 40 percent of the fund's cash distribution from its B units was taxed as interest income. The rest was received in the form of tax-advantaged dividends and capital gains (27.5 percent) or tax-deferred return of capital (32.5 percent). A 25 percent portfolio weighting for this or a similar fund would be all that is required to satisfy the 15 percent fixed-income target.

A non-registered portfolio (over age 50). For an older person, the same principles apply as for the previous portfolio, but risk should be reduced as retirement age approaches. As a broad rule of thumb, cut back the equity weighting by one percentage point for each year after age 50, until you reach 30 percent. So at age 60, the equity position would be down to a maximum of 40 percent. At age 70, the maximum would drop to 30 percent, where it would remain. The minimum equity exposure, no matter what your age or how conservative you are, should be in the 20 to 25 percent range.

Basic Sleep-Easy Non-Registered Portfolio (age 50 to 60)

Type of Security	Asset Class	Weighting (%)	Estimated Annual Return (%)
Money market fund or high-interest account	Cash	5	3.5
Investment-grade bonds	Fixed income	15	5
Preferred shares or funds	Variable income	10	5.5
REITs	Variable income	10	7
Conservative income funds	Variable income	20	7
Conservative Canadian equity funds	Growth	20	8
Conservative foreign equity funds	Growth	20	8
Total/average		100	6.87

This is how the portfolio would look at age 60, after a gradual reduction in the equity portion. The yield is lower, but we have reduced risk by reducing the equity weighting by 10 percentage points and switching it over to the income funds category, which will include a mix of various types of securities.

Basic Sleep-Easy Non-Registered Portfolio (age 60 to 70)

Type of Security	Asset Class	Weighting (%)	Estimated Annual Return (%)
Money market fund or high-interest account	Cash	5	3.5
Investment-grade bonds	Fixed income	15	5
Preferred shares or funds	Variable income	10	5.5
REITs	Variable income	15	7
Conservative income funds	Variable income	25	7
Conservative Canadian equity funds	Growth	15	8
Conservative foreign equity funds	Growth	15	8
Total/average		100	6.77

Here we see the portfolio as it might appear at age 70, with the equity portion down to 30 percent.

THESE PORTFOLIOS have each been set up in isolation. But they don't have to be treated that way if you have both registered and non-registered accounts. In that case, consider the two accounts as a single unit and shift assets to further maximize tax efficiency. Keep the tax-advantaged securities outside the RRSP or RRIF to obtain the maximum possible benefit. Just ensure that the overall asset allocation is on target.

Here's how this could work, using the basic RRSP and non-registered (under age 50) portfolios as examples.

Tax-Efficient Sleep-Easy RRSP Portfolio (under age 50)

Type of Security	Asset Class	Weighting (%)	Estimated Annual Return (%)
Money market fund or high-interest account	Cash	5	3.5
GICs	Fixed income	20	4.5
Stripped bonds	Fixed income	30	5
Bond funds or fixed-income ETFs	Variable income	10	5
Conservative income funds	Variable income	10	7
Conservative Canadian equity funds	Growth	12.5	8
Conservative foreign equity funds	Growth	12.5	8
Total/average		100	6.25

Tax-Efficient Sleep-Easy Non-Registered Portfolio (under age 50)

Type of Security	Asset Class	Weighting (%)	Estimated Annual Return (%)
Money market fund or high-interest account	Cash	5	3.5
Preferred shares or funds	Variable income	10	5.5
REITs	Variable income	10	7
Conservative income funds	Variable income	10	7
Conservative Canadian equity funds	Growth	32.5	8
Conservative foreign equity funds	Growth	32.5	8
Total/Average		100	6.97

All I have done is move the investment-grade bonds out of the non-registered portfolio and increase the weighting of the fixed-income portfolio of the RRSP accordingly. I reduced the equity funds weighting in the RRSP by a corresponding amount and added it to the non-registered portfolio. The result is that the bonds, which generate highly taxed interest income, are in the shelter of the RRSP. The equity funds produce capital gains and perhaps dividend income, so they work better for use in a non-registered portfolio.

This simple approach will maintain the overall target asset mix if the portfolios are approximately the same size. If the assets in each are significantly different, you'll need to make appropriate adjustments or the overall weighting will be distorted.

These sample portfolios are only general guidelines, but they provide a good starting point for your personal Sleep-Easy portfolio. Make adjustments appropriate to your situation. For example, an ultra-conservative investor may find that even my modest equity allocations are too high. Fine; move them down or even eliminate stocks entirely. But don't allow fear to override everything. Sure, you'll end up with a Sleep-Easy portfolio, but it may return less than 5 percent a year. Here's what such a portfolio might look like. I call it the Ultra-Soft Bed Portfolio.

The Ultra-Soft Bed Portfolio

Type of Security	Asset Class	Weighting (%)	Estimated Annual Return (%)
Money market fund or high-interest account	Cash	20	3.5
Laddered GICs	Fixed income	30	5.5
Short-term bond funds	Variable income	30	4
Universe bond funds	Variable income	20	5
Total/average		100	4.55

As you can see, you sacrifice a lot of yield for the high level of safety this portfolio provides. There is also no tax-efficiency here, since all the profits will be received as interest, so a portfolio such as this is best suited to a registered account. If you decide this type of portfolio is really what you want, use small financial institutions for the GICs and high-interest accounts so as to maximize yield. Keep your investments at any one institution to under $100,000 or whatever the maximum coverage of the applicable deposit insurance allows. Avoid the major banks because of the low rates they pay.

For the bond funds, choose no-load, low MER mutual funds, such as those offered by Phillips, Hager & North, or iShares units.

If you go this route, the only thing that may keep you awake is envy that other people are earning a lot more than you are when stocks are roaring ahead. But when markets are tumbling, you'll be content.

SLEEP-EASY ADVICE: Choose the portfolio model that is the best match for your goals and personality, and stick to it. You'll have comfortable nights for years to come.

Chapter 17

Last Words

However beautiful the strategy, you should occasionally look at the results.
—Winston Churchill

Sleep-Easy investing is more than just a money management philosophy; it is a lifestyle attitude. The true Sleep-Easy investor understands that while money is important, it is not the be-all and end-all of everything. The old adage tells us that money can't buy happiness. That may be true, but it can stave off a lot of misery. So the whole idea here is not the avoidance of money but, rather, its accumulation in ways that don't impinge on the more important priorities in life: family, health, job satisfaction, relaxation, and peace of mind.

The person who is obsessed with wealth will never be a Sleep-Easy investor because he or she will always be driven to make more. In doing so, compromises may be made, ranging from a high stress level to the abandonment of fundamental principles.

Fortunately, most people don't fall into that category. They have a realistic appreciation of money but aren't willing to sacrifice everything in its name. Recent social trends confirm this: More and more people are unwilling to work long hours and to spend an inordinate amount of time on the road at the cost of never seeing their children as they grow up.

The real problems in money management usually stem from the lack of a clear and consistent approach to the subject. We don't know how to spend, hence the huge debt loads many families are carrying. And we don't know how to save, which is why many people found themselves looking at shocking losses during the bear market.

What's required is self-discipline. People need a core reference point for dealing with money. You may not have thought much about it, but you probably base your decisions at work, at home, and in the community on a set of values that you have developed over your lifetime—your personal philosophy of life, as it were. For some people, the core reference is something clear and definable, such as a strong religious faith. For others, it is more nebulous. But we are all guided by certain basic rules imposed by society and by ourselves.

But not when it comes to money, it seems. Many people lack a proper frame of reference when it comes to matters financial. And without that frame of reference, they flounder.

Sleep-Easy investing is all about providing that centre point. I firmly believe that if you adopt my approach to looking after your money, the discipline that it requires will change your entire outlook and provide the direction that has been missing until now.

It's not a philosophy for everyone. It won't work for those who live for the thrill of the chase. But if you're one of the millions of Canadians who wants to build wealth without stress, this is the way to achieve that goal.

You don't have to accept it on blind faith. Try it out for a while and then, as Churchill suggested, look at the results—both in financial and personal terms. I think you'll like them.

Sleep well!

Sleep-Easy Q&As

Over the past couple of years I have received many questions from investors who are not sleeping easy and/or are contemplating actions that will put them into that stress-ridden group. Here is a selection; I've included my answers to each.

Repairing portfolio damage

Q. I am one lost puppy. I have managed to save $80,000, half in an RRSP and half outside. Right now about 30 percent is in cash. The investment advisor recommended—and I foolishly agreed to—some "less than stellar" funds two years ago. Thanks to your information, I am close to correcting this with my own selections; however, my two questions are as follows:

1. Is it worth it to pay the back-end sales fee (about $1,400 all together) to shift into better managed funds?
2. Should I even consider buying equity-based mutual funds right now or wait for the market to pull back?

A. This is exactly why I discourage people from using the back-end load (deferred sales charge or DSC) option. It locks you in. Unless you're willing to pay what amounts to a divorce fee, you're stuck in a fund for up to six years. However, there may be an out. See if you can find some better funds within the same company. If so, you can move into those without paying a DSC. And don't let the advisor hit you with a "switching fee" either—technically, they are allowed to charge up to 2 percent for a move.

Regarding your second question, I never encourage market timing. Who knows when stocks are going to pull back? If you are nervous about it, use a dollar-cost averaging approach and spread your investment commitments over several months (or longer).

"Tax-smart" RRIF withdrawals

Q. I just started withdrawing from my RRIF this January and recently heard there was a "tax-smart way" to withdraw those funds but was unable to obtain any details on that approach. I am simply taking the minimum amount out on a monthly basis based on my wife's age since she is a few years younger than I am. Could you please let me know if there is a more tax-efficient way to withdraw funds from an RRIF? Any other info you have on RRIF strategy would also be appreciated.

A. There are all kinds of angles for getting money out of RRIFs and RRSPs tax-free. Many are downright illegal (there have been prosecutions), while others, though legal, are simply gimmicky and involve high risk. One example is to create a leveraged non-registered portfolio and use the interest deduction that results to offset the RRIF or RRSP withdrawal. As you can see immediately, this just creates the illusion of a tax-free withdrawal. You still pay tax on the money coming out of the plan, plus you'll pay an after-tax interest cost on the portfolio loan. I don't like the whole idea.

Wants guaranteed 8 percent return

Q. I have $100,000 in an RRSP. Where can I get a rate of return of at least 8 percent on my investment and my investment is guaranteed?

0

A. Nowhere. Anyone who thinks this way has to stop dreaming and get real. If you want a true guarantee of both interest rate and return of capital, 4 to 5 percent is a much more realistic target. Beyond that, you will have to incur some risk, and the higher the desired return, the greater that risk will be. Anyone who claims to offer a guaranteed 8 percent these days is lying. If you look beneath the surface, you will certainly find there is risk involved.

Overcontributed by mistake

Q. I was an idiot and overcontributed to my 2007 RRSP. I thought it was fine to contribute the same amount as last year. My tax accountant informed me it wasn't fine, and I contributed $5,000 too much. I accomplished my boo-boo by transferring 200 shares of Royal Bank from my margin account to my RRSP account. I understand that I will be penalized by 1 percent per month on the extra $5,000. Is there a way I can transfer it back out and plead senility or something? Is there anything I can do to correct the mistake and ease the pain? I look forward to hearing from you. I've been a fan of yours for many years.

A. Yes, you have gotten yourself into a pickle. However, all is not lost. Here are four options to consider.
   1. Leave the money in the plan. You're allowed an overcon-tribution of $2,000, so you will only have to pay the penalty on $3,000, or $30 a month. That's $360 for a 12-month period, but as of next January 1st, you will be eligible for a new RRSP contribution, so you can apply the $3,000 against that and the penalty will end.
   2. File Form 3012A with the Canada Revenue Agency. Your accountant can handle it. This enables you to withdraw

the overcontribution from the plan without withholding tax. However, it may take six to eight weeks for the form to be processed.

3. If the transfer to the RRSP was made within the current month, see if the broker can reverse it.

4. Withdraw the money without using Form T3012A. Tax will be withheld, but the penalties will be avoided. The procedure for declaring this on your return is somewhat complicated, so ask your accountant to work it out for you.

Deciding on asset allocation

Q. My equity mutual funds have done well over the last few years and consequently my fixed-income asset allocation is now only approximately 40 percent. I have always felt it should be higher (50 percent?) because I am likely going to retire within five years with no pension. Every time I transfer a small amount of equity funds to my bond funds, the market does well and the bonds either stay flat or lose money and I kick myself for the money I lost. I have a similar problem in my RESP and in-trust accounts for my sons, which will be used within four years. Should I "Just Do It" or wait for a more consistent sign that the bear is here or that bond funds are improving?

A. One thing I have learned over the years is never, never try to outguess the market. It will always come back to haunt you. No one rings a bell to announce when a bull market begins or ends, and indexes can turn on a dime. Bonds add stability and safety to a portfolio, both important considerations for someone who is coming up to retirement and who is saving for her children's education. When you get frustrated, remember that people who had well-diversified portfolios with good bond holdings came through the 2000–02 bear market in much better shape than those who had everything in equities.

Having said that, a 40 percent position in fixed-income securities seems about right for someone in your situation. Rather than worry about moving more money into bonds, I suggest that you focus on making sure your equity funds are conservatively managed and carry low risk. See how they did during the bear.

Tax-free RRSP withdrawals

Q. According to a financial advisor we spoke to, you can melt down your RRSPs to avoid tax using a mutual fund with no margin call. What is a margin call? What is your opinion of this plan? What are the pros and cons? What risks are there with this idea?

A. A margin call suggests leverage—that means you are borrowing money from the brokerage firm to invest. "No margin call" simply means that if you suffer a heavy loss, the brokerage house won't demand that you put up more cash to cover it. The loss will simply be added to your debt (and of course will increase your interest expense).

It sounds to me like the plan being proposed is based on using borrowed money from the brokerage house to create a non-registered investment portfolio. The interest on the loan would be tax-deductible and therefore would presumably offset the tax payable on withdrawals from the RRSP.

In essence, you'll pay interest to the brokerage firm to save taxes on your RRSP. The net interest costs will likely be higher than any tax you save, and you'll be adding to your financial risk with a leveraged portfolio.

It's your decision but, frankly, I don't believe that someone who does not know the meaning of "margin call" should be involved in this kind of sophisticated manoeuvre.

Should she "fiddle" with tax return?

Q. I had a capital loss of $134.50 in 2006 on Shaw Communications. I bought the stock in January 2006 and sold it in July. Does having it less than a year pose a problem? Otherwise, I might fiddle it back to December 2005, since for $134 they are unlikely to check it out.

A. You might "fiddle it back"? What are you thinking? My advice is to never fiddle with the truth on your tax return. The Canada Revenue Agency has a very sophisticated computer system. The last thing you want is for them to start asking questions. And I guarantee that if they find one falsehood in your return, you'll be red-flagged for closer inspection in the future. In any event, there would be no reason to back-date your purchase. Unlike the United States, the CRA does not make a distinction between short-term and long-term capital gains and losses.

Tried to help son and got into trouble

Q. I have taken out a home equity loan of $50,000 to give to my son to help make a down payment on a new home for him and his wife (who is in med school).

I now find that I am required to repay my home equity loan at the rate of $1,500 per month. I did not expect it would be this much, as I had calculated repayment at about $600 per month, which I could handle. Now my problem is what I should do?

I have assets of $450,000, according to my bank. I am currently thinking that maybe I should cash in a $42,000

RRSP in order to reduce my home equity loan and subsequently my monthly payments to a more reasonable rate. What would be the drawbacks to this option and what if any kind of advice would you give me now that I am in this situation? My salary is only $50,000 per year and I have a home to maintain and pay taxes of $4,000 per year. Thank you.

A. Wow—what a mess! It's easy to say this in hindsight, but obviously you should have asked for confirmation of the monthly repayment rate before you made the decision to take the loan. It's a lesson for anyone contemplating a similar goodwill gesture.

I do not advise cashing in the RRSP. You'll be hit with tax at your marginal rate which, given your employment income, could be more than 40 percent on at least part of that amount. That's a hefty penalty to pay for a mistake.

Your first step should be to discuss the repayment schedule with the lender. A monthly payment of $1,500 on a $50,000 loan sounds excessive. Find out how it is calculated. At an interest rate of 8 percent (which is likely more than you are paying), that would mean the loan has been amortized over just three years. That makes no sense and leads me to believe there has been a miscalculation somewhere.

If the lender insists the figure is correct, then the simplest solution may be to convert the home equity loan, which I assume is in the form of a personal line of credit (PLC), into a conventional mortgage with a 25-year amortization. The financial institution that holds the PLC should be able to do this for you, since the loan presumably is already secured by the home. The monthly payment on a $50,000 mortgage loan over that period should be around $350, which you can certainly afford.

Wants to give royalties to kids

Q. I will get some royalty income on a book I authored, but I don't need the extra income. I am in the 33 percent marginal tax bracket and would like to give the income to my kids instead. Can I legally have the publishing company pay the royalties to my kids somehow, who are in med school and grad school, so that a third of the money doesn't go to the government?

A. Absolutely not, and the publisher would never agree to do such a thing, since it would amount to tax fraud. You are the author of the book, and the royalties must be paid to you and taxed accordingly. What you do with the money after that is your business.

   If you can show that your children contributed to the book in some way, perhaps through research, you could compensate them accordingly and claim a deduction for the expense. There should be proper paperwork documenting this.

For More Information

My company publishes three investment newsletters that followers
of my Sleep-Easy investing approach may find useful:

Internet Wealth Builder. This is our flagship publication, a
weekly email letter that is delivered each weekend. Top-flight
financial experts offer recommendations on a wide range of
securities, including Canadian, U.S., and international stocks,
mutual funds, bonds, preferred shares, trust units, and exchange-
traded funds.

The Income Investor. As the name suggests, the focus is on
income-producing securities. Our team looks at mutual funds,
trusts, high-yielding common stocks, preferred shares, split-share
units, and other revenue-generating choices. Special attention is
paid to the tax implications of all recommendations, and target
portfolios are published periodically. The emphasis is on lower-risk
securities. Frequency is twice monthly.

Mutual Funds Update. This was our first newsletter, and it is still
very popular with investors. We review a broad cross-section of
mutual funds and publish a quarterly Recommended List showing
our favourites and their current status. Many readers emulate our
three Ideal Portfolios—Safety, Balanced, and Growth—with excel-
lent results. Published monthly.

For full information on the newsletters and our other services, and to read free sample copies, please visit our website at www.buildingwealth.ca.

Endnotes

Chapter 4: The Twin Demons: Fear and Greed

1. Francis Chou, Chou Funds 1999 annual report.

Chapter 5: The Price of Ignorance

1. Northwater Market-Neutral Trust, 2006 annual report.

Chapter 6: Bubbles

1. Charles Mackay, *Extraordinary Popular Delusions and the Madness of Crowd* (1841; repr., New York: Harmony Books, 1980).
2. Ibid.
3. Ibid.
4. Technically, they actually hold only one-tenth of the shares they originally purchased. In 2006, Nortel consolidated its shares by issuing 1 new share for every 10 old ones.
5. Perhaps surprisingly, the Altamira e-business Fund still exists. However, by mid-2007 its total assets had been reduced to $13 million.
6. Mackay, *Extraordinary Popular Delusions.*

Chapter 7: Weighing Risk

1. FMF Capital Group prospectus, March 16, 2005.

Chapter 8: Hot Tip Nightmares

1. At that point, the company had changed its name to Brookfield Asset Management and the stock had split several times.
2. Superstar Stock Letter, November 10, 2004, http://osdir.com/ml/php.install/2004-11/msg00062.html.
3. Ontario Securities Commission, www.osc.gov.on.ca/Investor/Alert/ia_20021107_spam.jsp.
4. Ontario Securities Commission, www.osc.gov.on.ca/Investor/Alert/ia_20061207_spam-emails.jsp.

5. U.S. Securities and Exchange Commission, www.sec.gov/investor/ pubs/cyberfraud.htm.

6. Ibid.

Chapter 9: Get Rich—Go into Debt!

1. *Baldwin v. Daubney,* [2005] O.J. No. 5330 (S.C.J.).

2. www.osc.gov.on.ca/Investor/Resources/res_borrowing-to-invest_ en.pdf.

3. Disclosure: I was a spokesperson for the Canadian Home Income Plan, a reverse mortgage company, for several years. However, I no longer have any association with it.

Chapter 10: Sleep-Easy Tax Savings

1. *Helvering v. Gregory,* 69 F.2d 809 at 810–11 (2d Cir. 1934).

2. *Canada (Attorney General) v. Nash,* 2005 FCA 386.

3. Canada Revenue Agency, www.cra-arc.gc.ca/newsroom/alerts/2005/ a051110-e.html.

4. 2004 TTC 164 *Dubuc v. The Queen.*

5. Ernst & Young 2006 tax rates.

6. See www.fidelity.ca.

Chapter 11: The Retirement Follies

1. Canadian Institute of Actuaries, *Planning for Retirement: Are Canadians Saving Enough?* www.actuaries.ca/members/publications/2007/ Final%20CIA_Retirement_e.pdf.

2. Ibid.

3. For more on the subject, read my book *The Retirement Time Bomb,* published by Penguin Group (Canada) in 2005.

4. See www.tdcanadatrust.com/planning/rrsp_planning_calc.jsp.

Chapter 13: The Pursuit of Safety

1. See www.rbcroyalbank.com/cgi-bin/gic/rates/gic_return.cgi.

2. See www.ida.ca/Compliance/PPNGuidelines_en.asp.

Chapter 15: Choose Your Partners

1. HealthShares, www.healthsharesinc.com.

Acknowledgments

It was 20 years ago, in 1988, that I wrote my first financial book, *Building Wealth*. The publisher was Prentice Hall Canada. Since then, I have written or co-authored 17 money-related books, not counting the annual guides to RRSPs and mutual funds that were published for 15 years, from 1989 to 2004. With a couple of exceptions, all of those books were published by Prentice Hall and its successor companies. The imprint is now Penguin Group (Canada), but several of the key people are the same folks I worked with at Prentice Hall. I owe them an enormous debt of gratitude for the encouragement and support they have given me over these many years, and I want to publicly thank them here.

I am particularly grateful to my editor-in-chief, Andrea Magyar, who has always kept me on track and provided many valuable suggestions and insights over the years. Andrea also strongly supported me when I suggested moving in a different direction with the *Quizmas* books. There are now three of them, and it has been a delight (and a great change of pace) to work with my daughter Deborah in writing them.

I also want to extend my thanks to Judy Phillips, my copy editor on this book, and Chandra Wohleber, the production editor who looked after all of the many details involved in bringing a project like this to reality. Also, thank you to the Penguin Group (Canada) staff who participated in the design, promotion, and marketing of this and my previous books.

My wife tells me that this should be my last investment book. "Take some time off and enjoy yourself," she says. Perhaps I will. But as J.K. Rowling said when she was begged to write more Harry Potter books: "Never say never." So I'll simply say: "No more, at least for a while."

Finally, thanks to all the readers who have shown an interest in my work over the years. I hope I have helped make your financial life a little easier.

For now, so long.

Index